THE FIFTEENTH-CENTURY BOOK

PUBLICATIONS OF THE A. S. W. ROSENBACH
FELLOWSHIP IN BIBLIOGRAPHY

THE FIFTEENTH-CENTURY BOOK

THE SCRIBES ❧ THE PRINTERS ❧ THE DECORATORS

by Curt F. Bühler A. S. W.

ROSENBACH FELLOW IN BIBLIOGRAPHY

PHILADELPHIA
UNIVERSITY OF PENNSYLVANIA PRESS

For TAHN *with love*

Foreword

THE PRESENT VOLUME contains the substance of the three lectures given at the University of Pennsylvania on the ninth, sixteenth, and twenty-third of April, 1959, as part of the A. S. W. Rosenbach Fellowship in Bibliography. I should like to thank the Selection Committee for the honor which is implied by the invitation to hold this Fellowship.

The text of the lectures has, here and there, been very slightly modified, and a few additions (chiefly statistics, unsuited for oral delivery) have been made. On the whole, however, the material here printed is substantially the same as that given in the lectures. The notes have provided an opportunity to supply some further information which, it is hoped, will explain and strengthen the points made in the text proper.

As always, it is a pleasure to express my warm thanks to those who have helped in the preparation of this work. My deepest gratitude must go to my wife, who once again has patiently read, criticized, and improved the text as it went through its several revisions. The continuing interest and generous cooperation of Professors Kenneth M. Setton and Ru-

FOREWORD

dolf Hirsch of the University of Pennsylvania should receive special mention. I should also like to give sincere thanks to my colleagues at the Pierpont Morgan Library, who have always been willing to advise me. Finally, I am indebted to The Times (of London) and to The New York Times for permission to use the quotations appearing on pp. 110 and 161.

Benigne lector: Ignoscas aliquot erroribus
vel machinae vel calami!

C. F. B.

Contents

Plates

PLATES

THE FIFTEENTH-CENTURY BOOK

I
THE SCRIBES

HE FIFTEENTH CENTURY, it may well be said, was one of the most curious and confused periods in recorded history, containing within it elements of both the old and the new, the last flowering of the mediaeval world and the beginnings of our own modern age. Not the least curious and confusing of its aspects is the story of the book production in that century and of the truly amazing development in the printing industry within the short span of fifty years. The historic event of the invention of printing has given rise to a really astonishing amount of flatly self-contradictory speculation and theorizing; an examination of these contradictions will be one of the chief concerns of this series of lectures.

The fifteenth century, then, was an anomalous period, and it abounded in anomalies. Let me illustrate this with the description of a volume in my own small library of fifteenth-century books. This volume includes the text of the familiar *Poeniteas cito,* which here occupies fifty-four leaves of vellum. The quires are signed a-f ^{8} g^6 with catch-words for each quire and with running heads providing a clue as to the section of the text on the leaf. The work is provided with a fine large initial at its incipit, in blue and red, recalling the work of Peter Schoeffer; the volume is also rubricated and contains spaces elsewhere for the insertion of large initials by the illuminator. The colophon reads in translation: "This present work 'de modo confitendi et poenitendi' was completed in the sprightly city of Antwerp by me, Gerard Leeu, on 8 January

1486." The textual extracts cited by Hain-Copinger 11495,[1] Campbell 1130, and Polain 3219[2] agree practically verbatim with the readings in my volume, if the date be corrected to January 28th.[3]

When I suggest that I would very much like to know something about the man who produced this volume, some one will be sure to remark that we do indeed know a good deal about the printer, Gerard Leeu.[4] Indeed we do—but the trouble is that the volume which I have just been describing was, in fact, never printed and consequently was not, in all probability, produced by Leeu. It is a manuscript. A score of years ago, I described this as "An Unusual Fifteenth-century Manuscript";[5] the only unusual thing about this was the truly magnificent display of my own ignorance. As I now know, a very considerable number of such manuscripts, copied from printed books, have survived into our day[6]—and experience has taught me that every manuscript ascribed to the second half of the fifteenth century is potentially (and often without question) a copy of some incunable. Our knowledge of palaeography being what it is, this circumstance can also apply to manuscripts believed to have been written before 1450!![7] This is a topic to which we shall return at a later time. For the present, it may be sufficient to say that we have now ventured into that no man's land which is supposed, quite erroneously, to lie between the worlds of the written and printed books.[8] Actually, of course, there is very little real difference between the fifteenth-century manuscripts and the incunabula—and the student of the earliest printing would be well advised if he viewed the new invention, as the first printers did, as simply another form of writing—in this case, "artificialiter scribere."[9]

There are prevalent, nonetheless, some very curious mis-

16

conceptions about the value and importance of manuscripts as compared with printed books.[10] Every manuscript is, quite obviously, unique—but it does not follow therefrom that every manuscript has textual value or intellectual significance. Contrariwise, the vast majority of the incunables exist in multiple copies—but it does not therefore follow that the editions surviving in a score or more of copies are not of prime importance and signal value for their texts. Indeed, ignorance and carelessness of scribes[11]—a subject which called forth the vehement wrath[12] of such diverse personages as Cicero,[13] Strabo,[14] Roger Bacon,[15] Petrarch,[16] Leonardo Bruni,[17] Chaucer,[18] and Bishop Reginald Pecock[19]—together with the uniqueness and consequent cost of the hand-written book, represent the chief drawbacks in the production of books prior to the discovery of the art of exactly reproducing a practically unlimited number of identical copies. When Rabelais affirmed the doctrine "Cela est escrit. Il est vray," he reflected, if anything, faith in the author, not in the scribe.

Towards the turn of the century, it was still true, as Caxton reminds us even so late as 1481, that "wordes ben perisshyng, vayne, & forgeteful, and writynges duelle & abide permanent." [20] It is, of course, a commonplace observation that the production of books was an established and flourishing industry long before the introduction of the printing press.[21] The length of time that it took to produce these volumes may well have been a limiting factor in the availability of manuscripts; the scarcity of books throughout the manuscript era was heavily stressed by Wilhelm Wattenbach in his learned and fascinating handbook.[22] Roberto Weiss, on the other hand, argues that there must have been plenty of manuscripts for sale, at least in the Italy of the fifteenth century, as is evidenced by the purchases of Duke Humphrey of Gloucester and of the many other English humanists, who flocked to the Peninsula in those years. Indeed, we have complaints that the English visitors fairly denuded the country of manuscripts, to the great sorrow of local and transalpine scholars.[23] Whether available or not,[24] there can be little question but that manuscripts were expensive.[25] The dream of the Clerk of Oxenford was to possess twenty books; he would rather have had them than rich robes (a thread-bare courtepy sufficed him) or a fiddle or a psaltery[26] —but Chaucer does *not* tell us that he actually possessed so many, even if this figure merely represents a round number. All authorities agree,[27] however, that manuscripts cost a great deal of money in their own day (let alone today!!), and it comes as no surprise that, in Chaucer's story,[28] Jankyn fetched Alison such a clout over the head that she became deaf in one ear. She had committed the heinous crime of tearing a leaf out of his book! Perhaps to the contrary, we may nevertheless be forced to conclude that even such a hack writer as the anonymous author of the *Court of Sapience* must have had access to a very considerable library in order to turn out that "literary mosaic" which serves as his monument.[29] If an author needed to acquire such a library, it is self-evident that, in those days, manuscripts could be obtained either by purchase or through copying. The several ways of procuring them are best exemplified, perhaps, by the Monk Thorirus Andreae[30] who wrote, had written for him, bought as is, and assembled by purchase from several booksellers[31] the manuscripts which he collected while attending the Council of Constance.

If the scarcity and cost of manuscripts limited the size of individual libraries, this in turn limited the size of institutional ones, which depended for growth on the gift and bequeathal of books by the several scholars.[32] In Italy, of course, where manuscripts were most readily to be found, large libraries were the privilege of the wealthy and the powerful.[33] But even here, a manuscript was a sort of luxury commodity,[34] it having been estimated that a typical vellum manuscript of the fifteenth century, in finished form and bound, cost between seven and ten ducats; this equalled a month's wages for the average official at the Neapolitan court.[35] Elsewhere, the situation was even more desperate—and few individual scholars possessed what would have been a large library fifty to a hundred years later. At Cambridge,[36] the University Library, we are informed, owned a mere 122 volumes in 1424—and after another half-century, the total had only reached 330 books. The inventory of Clare College, of about the year 1440, lists 111 items.[37] In 1481, when John Warkeworth presented fifty-four manuscripts to the library, Peterhouse owned a total of 439 works, of which only 200 have survived there.[38] From its founder (Robert Woodlarke), St. Catharine's received eighty-seven manuscripts about the year 1473, none of which are still on the library shelves of that college.[39] In France, too, manuscripts were hardly commonplace.[40] King Charles VIII appears to have owned only some 130 volumes, the thirty coming to him upon the death of his father (Louis XI), the rest having belonged to his mother.[41] Manuscripts also disappeared from the shelves of the French Royal library, and 188 volumes mentioned in 1373 were no longer there in 1411.[42] Books may have been expensive, but little care seems to have been taken for their safe-guarding. This loss of manuscripts given or bequeathed to public institutions is one of the sorriest happenings in the history of libraries.[43] It has been suggested that, with the advent of printed books, manuscripts came to be regarded as

19

obsolete and superfluous and were therefore discarded.[44] Abbot
Johann Tritheim, it will be recalled, shrewdly exchanged
printed books for manuscripts belonging to clerics who, as he
stated, "owned but either did not understand or were afraid
of" these profane volumes.[45] In 1550, the Imperial court-
historian Nicolaus Mameranus bewailed the fact that many
monasteries had sold off or had given away their manuscripts
when they received printed versions of these texts.[46] In any
event, so far as private libraries were concerned, it was not till
the closing years of the fifteenth century that the satirist
Sebastian Brant could justifiably wave an admonitory finger
at the "book-fool" whom he berated for his "tum librorum
multitudine tum diversa scribentium varietate." [47] For centuries before this, books were chiefly owned by institutions, the
individual owner being the exception.[48]

Manuscripts, naturally, could be produced by anyone who
could write—that is, by every one who belonged to the literate
community.[49] Such book production, therefore, resulted either
from the work of a professional scribe or from the activity of an
amateur. It seems to me that the contribution of the latter class
has, in general, been overlooked, though it is clear that the
number of "occasional" scribes, who wrote for themselves as
well as for others, could hardly have been smaller than the
total of the professional scriveners.[50] A list at the Pierpont
Morgan Library, compiled by John Baglow of our staff,[51]
records no fewer than 2058 individuals who signed their names
to the manuscripts they had written—a list drawn in large
part from three sources only. There are numerous names here
unknown to John W. Bradley, who provides 2380 entries
(as I have counted them),[52] and this includes many persons
whose connection with the production of manuscripts was

slight in the extreme, since Bradley included patrons, artists, printers, authors, and the like. But the surprising thing as regards the actual writers is that there are so many names[53] which can be identified with only a single manuscript.[54] These must have been occasional scribes indeed, even when one assumes the loss of other manuscripts of theirs which have not survived into the twentieth century. And yet a significant number of these manuscripts are very fine ones, judged worthy to take their place in such libraries as those formed by Dyson Perrins,[55] Sir Sydney Cockerell,[56] and other fastidious collectors.

Each country, of course, had its professional scribes,[57] engaged in the mass production of manuscripts,[58] and their names are known to us—Vespasiano da Bisticci,[59] Diebold Lauber,[60] Ludwig Hennflin,[61] and John Shirley[62] come to mind.[63] But scriptoria are also known to have existed of whose personnel we know nothing—specifically the one in Strassburg[64] which produced at least ten surviving manuscripts between 1418 and 1421 and that London bookshop about which Professor Laura Loomis has written.[65] Incidentally, it should be recalled that the calligraphically most beautifully executed manuscripts, which without exception come from the hand of a professional scribe, often contain the worst texts.[66] The scribes equally often excused themselves for this or apologized in such subscriptions as: "Qui leget emendat, scriptorem non reprehendat" and "Si erravit scriptor, debes corrigere, lector." [67] In all fairness, however, one can also cite contrary evidence and recall here that the finest manuscript of the *Canterbury Tales*, the Ellesmere manuscript now in the Huntington Library, provides the best authority for Chaucer's classic work.[68]

The ranks of the professional writers were also augmented by the "semipros"—university students who copied texts for others and thus helped to work their way through the university, a financial solution for the costs of education which is often thought to be a modern expedient.[69] Lay writers like the "Stuhlschreiber," who flourished in Dresden until 1820 and in the Orient (of course) into our own day, even included women in their ranks; one may mention, in this connection, a certain Clara Hätzlerin of Augsburg, who copied texts for payment in the years 1452-1476.[70]

Nuns, too, are known to have written manuscripts, and a sister Elisabeth Warrüszin, the writer of a *Life of St. Catherine* which (at least before the War) was preserved in Berlin, may be cited as an example.[71] This, in turn, brings us to the monastic scriptoria; following a decline in activity in the preceding centuries, these seem to have taken a new lease on life towards the end of the fourteenth century, a renaissance which extended into the following one. A new scriptorium was built, for example, at the monastery of St. Albans, not far from London, in the time of Abbot Thomas de la Mare (1349-1396).[72] We know for certain that the Dominicans had no fewer than thirty-one scribes known to us by name who were working at Basel at the time of the Council (1431-1449).[73] So late as 1492, Abbot Andreas renewed the scriptorium at Kloster Berge near Magdeburg.[74] Such examples as these amply testify to the useful activity of the monastic scriptorium in the fifteenth century.

The professional production of manuscripts was dwarfed, I am convinced, by the quantity of books produced by the enterprise which, for want of a better term, one may call the "every man his own scribe" movement. There was nothing, of course, to prevent anyone from writing his own manuscripts[75] —and most of the people with scholarly attainments unquestionably did do so.[76] It is well known that Petrarch[77] copied texts and wrote out those of his own poems,[78] though he also had copies made for him and employed his own scribe.[79] In this connection, however,[80] one should recall the words of Zomino da Pistoia who wrote in his Cicero: "Melius est emere libros iam scriptos quam scribi facere—It is better to buy books already written than to have them written out." [81] This statement brings to mind the present-day adage that "fools build houses for other people to live in." Cardinal Nicolaus Cusanus was not above copying manuscripts,[82] and Chaucer, both in his professional capacity and as author, must have done a lot of writing, though he too employed his own scribe.[83] The English humanists—such as Robert Flemmyng,[84] John Free, John Goolde, John Gunthorpe, and others[85]—certainly made transcriptions for their own use. Nor was this activity confined to the British Isles, for we find, for example, the wealthy Augsburg citizen Georg Mülich writing out a *Chronicle* of his native city,[86] while Vespasiano da Bisticci tells us that Lapo di Castiglionchi transcribed many of his Latin and Greek books.[87] He regretfully adds the true bookseller's observation that Lapo was "a poor man"—and therefore was presumably obliged to demean himself with this sort of labor. Transalpine students were notoriously impecunious— and, for that matter of fact, so too were German professors,[88] for these are known to have copied books well into the sixteenth century.[89] The Italian scholars were financially better off and they could afford, on occasion, to hire scribes to work for them. Thus, in 1475, the Sicilian student Alfonso Diodemate contracted with the Neapolitan copyist Jacopo de Aulesa to write out for him ("in carta di coiro") the commentary by Albertus Magnus on Aristotle's *Physics*.[90] Some scribes, working for themselves, managed to build up quite respectable libraries for their own use. Such a man was Johann Sintram of Würzburg,[91] who in 1444 (six years before his death) presented no fewer than sixty-one manuscripts to the library of the Franciscans in his native city. He was indefatigable in his copying, working at Würzburg, Ulm, Reutlingen, Esslingen, Strassburg, Colmar, Oxford, and, I dare say, at other places as well. As befits this methodical gatherer of texts, many of his volumes were "Sammelbände," containing numerous short tracts by various authors and brought together to suit Sintram's personal tastes.

Suddenly, at mid-century and (so far as the writers were concerned) quite unexpectedly, the printing press appeared upon the scene and thrust its way into the well-ordered and non-competitive way of life in which the scribes prepared their wares.[92] What effect did this have upon the scribes and their means of livelihood? [93] One thing must be borne in mind—and that is the fact that, in the strata of society which made its living through its ability to write, only a relatively small proportion were book-scribes. The vast majority, it is manifest, pursued their chosen career in the courts (both judicial [94] and aristocratic),[95] the chanceries, the archives, and in the other offices of government and, so far as it then went, of commerce. This group was left quite undisturbed by the advent of the new invention. Indeed, they continued to ply their trade in the same way they had always done until the introduction, in the late nineteenth century, of modern business machines. But even the IBM has been unable to put an end to scribal endeavors—and today many artists are still able to make a career for themselves by their competence with the pen. As late as the 1920s, I am told, newcomers to the staff of the Bodleian Library had to learn a standard, prescribed hand, so that a certain uniformity of entry could be maintained.[96] Here may well be seen the last flowering of the mediaeval writing-masters.

As for what happened to the book-scribe, it was the fashion, some years ago, to hold that the press promptly put them out of business.[97] This was a belief that the contemporary printer also fostered, although professional pride has often been the parent of wishful thinking. The early Lyonese printer, Johann Trechsel,[98] proclaimed that block-printing had little effect upon the scribes, but that the introduction of printing by means of movable types wrote "finis" to their careers and forced them to learn how to bind if they did not wish to become mendicants. In 1916, George Barwick expressed the view that, in the year 1470, there were, in France alone, some six thousand "writers solely occupied in transcribing manuscripts," and that ten years later this total had been reduced to a mere handful.[99] In 1952, this view still found its adherents.

Such an opinion, however, seems wholly unwarranted to me. Anyone at all acquainted with the large collections of mediaeval manuscripts—or who has perused the printed catalogues of such accumulations—knows for a fact that nearly as many manuscripts written in the second half of the fifteenth century have come down to us as of those which are judged to belong to the first half-century.[100] Further, it seems most improbable that the proportional relationship between what was written and what has survived would differ materially for these closely related periods. I heartily concur in the estimate that "the impact of that invention [printing] on the

25

lives of professional writers was less immediate, less mortal than has been generally supposed." [101] Two Italian scholars (Mariano Fava and Giovanni Bresciano) similarly remark: "I copisti continuarono, anche dopo l'introduzione della stampa, ad esercitare con profitto la loro professione." [102] They served not only the powerful and the wealthy, but even supplied the needs of the "umili studiosi," at least in Italy. It would seem likely that manuscripts and incunabula were successful in achieving a sort of peaceful co-existence, [103] the hoped-for ideal of these later days in the political sphere. The former provided what was distinct and personal, [104] while the latter supplied the accurate, useful texts which scholars needed, and at a price which even a German cleric could afford.

What, then, became of the book-scribes? What happened to the various categories of writers of literary works, who practiced their trade prior to 1450, once the printing press was established? The professionals previously employed by the large scriptoria seem to have done no more than to change their titles and thereupon became calligraphers; [105] in any event, they went right on doing what had been their task for centuries. On the one hand, it should be remembered that calligraphers necessarily catered principally, if not exclusively, to the "de luxe-bespoke" trade. On the other, it was not apparent until the very late fifteenth century—or more fully, perhaps, in the sixteenth—that calligraphy had turned into an applied art or, at worst, a mere hobby. [106] The scriptoria themselves seem to have been unable to compete with the printing firms and the publishing houses which subsequently came into being—although some managed to survive by becoming booksellers. Their employees, however, enjoyed a variety of alternate choices, [107] in that they could contrive to attach themselves to well-to-do patrons,[108] to carry on a bespoke trade,[109] or to become the itinerant scribes (mostly of Germanic or of Low Country origin) who wandered all over Europe in these years, even working in Italy.[110] Some scribes[111] joined forces with the enemy and became printers themselves—though some of those upon whom Fortune did not smile later forsook the press and returned to their former occupation. This is rather strong evidence for the belief that a scribe, in the closing years of the fifteenth century,[112] could still make a living for himself with his pen.[113] Occasionally, it almost seems as if the scriveners themselves took to publication; this alone may account for the five manuscripts of Diogenes Cynicus which the scribe Giovanni Marco Cinico of Parma ("Velox," as he liked to call himself) is known to have written—at least that number of them has survived.[114] At this time, too, booksellers (a certain Maistre Vatos of Lille may be cited) [115] probably commissioned scribes to write manuscripts for their stock, in the firm expectation that they could sell them to individuals without difficulty.

The monastic scriptoria, certainly in Germany, seem to have met the competition of the press with greater success than their commercial colleagues enjoyed. Abbot Konrad V of Tegernsee actively encouraged the production of manuscripts in the years 1461 to 1492,[116] while the Kremsmünster scriptorium flourished under Ulric Schoppenzaun in 1454-1484.[117] The monastery at Benediktbeuern, from 1495 to 1510, made large purchases of vellum and paper, which were obviously intended for book-production.[118] Numerous Missals were engrossed in Salzburg in the score of years following 1470,[119] while at Augsburg, as late as 1595, Frater Dreer was still writing his "Chorbücher." [120] A most important development for the manuscript market of the fifteenth century was the founding of the order of the "Fratres vitae communis." [121] The late E. Ph. Goldschmidt [122] has estimated that perhaps a fourth of all the books produced in that century can, one way or another, be connected with this movement. The Brothers of the Common Life wanted the books to be spread throughout the populace, not merely to be preserved "apud paucos in conclavis," [123] and with this end in view, they made use of the press as well as the pen. The monastic scriptoria, then, continued a healthy existence—but it must be remembered that they, as opposed to those who had to make a living out of their writing, were not *primarily* operating for profit, though (one may be sure) no profit was refused.

In the second half of the Quattrocento, those who could afford to do so retained scribes on their payrolls, even as their colleagues of the decades before the invention of printing had done. That the demand for their services exceeded the supply of scribes is shown by Niccolò Michelozzi's complaint to Naldo de Naldis, in September 1465, concerning the paucity of copyists. [124] Still, William Gray, Bishop of Ely, not only had the scribe Theoderick Werken busily copying manuscripts for him but also employed another German copyist, a certain Reynbold. [125] Further, Gray used his secretary, Richard Bole, in this capacity (cf. Balliol MS. 78a) and also had at least one manuscript written for him by the Italian Niccolò Perotti (MS. Urb. lat. 1180). Sir John Fastolf [126] may well have required his secretary, William Worcester, to act as a copyist, in addition to the multitudinous other duties which the niggardly old knight demanded of him. Since he also had manuscripts written for him in French at a time when Worcester was still receiving instruction in that language (in 1458), [127] it follows

28

that Fastolf, who died in the following year, must have used other scribes as well. In Germany, Johann Wernher, Freiherr zu Zimbern, hired the scribe Gabriel Lindennast to write manuscripts for his library, printed books being so inferior.[128] Both the Bentivoglio of Bologna and the Aragonese court at Naples continued to employ scribes after 1450,[129] and the Vatican scriptors still turned out books in the second half of the Cinquecento; Ferdinando Ruano, between 1551 and 1553, prepared at least five manuscripts for the Papal library, while in 1556-1558, Gianfrancesco Cresci produced both vellum and paper codices for the Vatican.[130] Federigo III of Montefeltro, the Duke of Urbino who died on 10 September 1482, not only bought manuscripts in wholesale lots from the bookseller Vespasiano da Bisticci, but he also had his librarian Veterano transcribe books for him.[131] In the 1560s, Heinrich Rüdinger was writing out texts for his lord,[132] the Pfalzgraf Ottheinrich of such unpleasant appearance. You may recall that this Count Palatine referred to himself as "monstrum hominis potius quam homo—a monster of a man rather than a man."

Skilled writers also carried on a bespoke trade after the invention of the press, in the tradition of Vespasiano. English royalty and its aristocracy turned to Bruges[133] and other continental cities for their "de luxe" volumes. Thus, Edward IV purchased from Flanders the French text of Boccaccio's *Fall of Princes* and the *Recueil des histoires de Troye,* though in each case it seems likely that the printed editions of these texts, produced by Colard Mansion and William Caxton in Bruges itself, were already on the market at that time.[134] King Henry VIII and Henry Fitzalan, Earl of Arundel, commissioned continental scribes resident in England to prepare luxury volumes

29

for them.[135] Competent English scribes, too, found customers among the nobility, as the interesting *Horae* written for Thomas Butler, 7th Earl of Ormond, bears witness (MS Royal 2 B XV). In 1487, the Duke of Calabria (to cite but one Italian example) ordered from the scribe Giovan Rainaldo a vellum *Croniche di Napoli*.[136]

Leonhard Wagner (born in Augsburg in 1454) [137] wrote some forty-nine manuscripts according to his own list. He wrote mostly for his own monastery but occasionally also for others, including the Emperor Maximilian. Wagner's most famous work is the *Proba centum scripturarum,* a manual containing a hundred different hands, which is preserved in two manuscripts. About half the forms of handwriting displayed in this treatise were historic and were not used in the fifteenth or sixteenth century in Augsburg or elsewhere. Further, the contents of his manuscripts were mediaeval in character, whether he was writing in a "new" hand or not. In Leonhard Wagner, then, we see the transition from scribe to calligrapher.

During the fifteenth century, two sorts of books still required to be written by hand *in any case,* whenever there was a demand for them. First of all, printing in Greek had not yet attained the stature, prior to 1490, with which Aldus Manutius and Johann Froben were to invest it in the decades following. True, there was some Greek printing,[138] but it was limited in quantity and, with but few exceptions, inferior in appearance and in text. Greek scribes, and Italian ones proficient in the writing of Greek,[139] continued throughout the century to find a practically unlimited market for their products, and one finds them working not only for Italian customers but also in France (one may cite George Hermonymus of Sparta) [140] and in England (for example, John Serbopoulos and Emanuel of Constantinople).[141] Even at the very fringes of the civilized world, according to the views of the day, there was a demand for Greek manuscripts. In the third quarter of the fifteenth century, the Hungarian Bishop of Pécs (Fünfkirchen, as it was known in German), Bishop Janus III Pannonius left money in Italy to pay for the transcription of Greek texts which he did not already possess.[142] Scribes not only did work for others, they also wrote for themselves; in this connection notice should be taken of Demetrius Trivolis[143] who, in Corfu, Crete and Rome, wrote at least seven manuscripts in the years 1462-1481, five of which have the note that they were "his work and his property." Greek codices have survived to our day copied out by the most distinguished and erudite of humanists: Erasmus, Il Codro, Ficino, Filelfo, Budé, and Estienne may be singled out here.[144] Bartolomeo Zanetti of Castrezzato, near Brescia, in the first half of the Cinquecento, printed Greek texts in Florence, Rome, and Venice; however, he also worked as a copyist in the production of Greek manuscripts under the name of Βαρθολομαῖος Βριξιανός.[145]

In addition to the Greek texts, there were Latin ones which had not yet appeared in print either because their subject matter was unfit or unsuited for publication or because the potential sale of these works was deemed too limited to warrant setting them up in type. When additional copies of texts not yet in print were needed, they had, of course, to be duplicated by hand. Manuscripts of goliardic[146] or of satyric verse[147] that attacked vested interests,[148] rare theological and didactic tracts such as that by Vigilius, the fifth-century Bishop of Thapsus,[149] and Simon Islip's *Tractatus de gubernacione regni* (written for Edward III),[150] local chronicles like those of William of Malmesbury and of Henry of Huntington,[151] service books for a remote diocese—such works had to be copied out afresh when more examples were needed, since these texts had not yet enjoyed the dignity of passing through the press. Thus, in 1488, the Aragonese court at Naples paid the scribe Giovanni de Frandena twelve ducats for preparing a vellum copy of the *De mirabili scientia dei* (better known as the *Summa theologiae*) by Albertus Magnus.[152] No fifteenth-century edition of this text is known to the authoritative *Gesamtkatalog der Wiegendrucke.*

On the other hand, one cannot help wondering, on occasion, as to *why* a scholar required a certain manuscript to be written for him. Thus, Pico della Mirandola had a copy of Pliny's *Natural History* made which is dated 17 August 1481.[153] At that time, no fewer than eight editions had been printed. Could all of these have been "out-of-print" already? The scribe who was just mentioned, Giovanni de Frandena, in 1492, wrote for the court of Ferdinando "il Bastardo" of Naples an *Opera* of Alexander de Hales,[154] despite the fact that a complete edition of the *Summa* had been printed in Pavia[155] three years earlier.[156] Though already printed at Bologna in 1481,[157] so extensive a work as the *Super epistolas Pauli* of St. Thomas Aquinas was written out, presumably in Flanders in the years 1491-1493, and filled three large vellum volumes.[158] As the fifteenth century drew to its close, a very considerable number of quite inferior *Books of Hours* were turned out in direct competition with the very fine printed editions of these devotional books which were the specialty of Parisian printers.

At this time, too, there was no apparent slackening of activity on the part of the scholars who wrote books for their own use or entertainment.[159] Characteristic of such activity was that of the two humanists from Nuremberg, Hartmann Schedel and his much older cousin Hermann.[160] On their visits to Italy, both made numberless copies of texts which they needed or wanted, these manuscripts being now mostly in the Bayerische Staatsbibliothek. Readers, of course, continued to use manuscripts and incunabula indifferently; quotation and reference to texts unpublished, so far as we are aware, imply the continued use of the hand-written book into the late Quattrocento.[161] Those manuscripts of the period which repose on the shelves of the great national libraries in the countless hundreds, and which are never to be seen in the display cases of their exhibition rooms,[162] were mostly written by anonymous scholars in connection with their own studies. Yet these manuscripts were not only written—they were also bought, sold, and exchanged, for the "littera scripta" still kept its honored place "on shelves couched at his beddes heed" as with Chaucer's Clerk Nicholas.[163] The trade in books throughout the Middle Ages, it needs scarcely to be stressed, was largely a second-hand business;[164] only with the invention of printing did a new-book market become commonplace.

When, in the face of innumerable editions, both cheap and expensive in array, one notes texts of such authors as Aristotle, Catullus, Cicero, Horace, Juvenal, Martial, Persius, Seneca and Vergil written out almost at the turn of the century (and sometimes even later),[165] one cannot help but be puzzled by their very existence. A calligraphic text was, of course, the prerogative of the wealthy, but the routine, prosaic copy of a classic can only be accounted for on the basis that, as the fifteenth century was dying, it still was more economical to write out your own manuscript than to buy a printed version, even a second-hand one. It is recorded that Abbot Wolfgang von

33

Reun (1481-1515) himself wrote many books and made sumptuous volumes of his writings, perhaps with more vainglory than one should expect to find in a monk.[166] Sometimes, too, such writing out of books became a labor of love. Thus the librarian of Kloster Vorau, Johann Antonius Zunggo, when an old man, wrote out Hymnals for the use of his monastery; they are said to be large volumes, finely written and handsomely decorated. Zunggo died at the age of eighty-five years —in 1775.[167]

The circumstances here noted provide, I assume, some explanation for the existence of manuscript copies of printed books, to which reference was made at the beginning of this address. Some years ago, I published a list of a score of manuscripts which derive directly from Caxton printings;[168] to this I can now add Peterhouse, Cambridge, MS. 190, a copy of the 1482 *Chronicles of England*.[169] Printings by Wynkyn de Worde and the *Book of St. Albans* underwent similar treatment.[170] A copy was made of John Mirk's *Festial* from the text as printed at Rouen by Martin Morin, 22 June 1499; the scribal slips in the colophon ("Tinctum" for "Finitum," and "primi" for "Iunii") give strong testimony for the scribe's lack of training, learning, or attention—perhaps, indeed, of all three.[171] Copying from time to time became quite slavish,[172] as, for example, in St. John's, Cambridge, MS. 178.[173] Although the descriptive catalogue does not point this out, this vellum manuscript is a copy of an edition of Johannes Nider's *Consolatorium timoratae conscientiae* put out in Paris by that ex-juvenile delinquent Pierre Le Dru, 31 January 1494.[174] The manuscript has the *same* collation, the *same* number of lines to the page, and the *identical* colophons;[175] it is, therefore, a close, perhaps even an exact, page-for-page facsimile of the incunable.[176]

Such work may possibly be explained in the light of the opinion expressed by Abbot Johann Tritheim,[177] when he wrote: "Truly if writing is set down on vellum, it will last for a millennium. When printing is on paper, however, how long will it last? It would be much if printing in a paper volume were to survive for two hundred years." The judgment of the worthy Abbot, as we now know, was faulty, since the paper of five hundred years ago seems as sturdy and crisp today as ever it was. However, Tritheim's zeal in exhorting his scribes to copy on vellum the printed texts ("impressos utiles per scripturam perpetuare") was most commendable.[178]

Hartmann Schedel, as every one no doubt is aware, copied many printed editions (mostly of Italian origin) for his library,[179] but it is not quite so evident why he did this, since he came of a family that was very wealthy. It has been suggested that Schedel made his transcriptions because he could not procure from Italy the editions themselves—but in that case where did he obtain the prototypes for the copies he made?

A circumstance which seems to defy explanation is that of the five existing manuscripts of Ermolao Barbaro's *Oratio ad Fridericum III Imperatorem et Maximilianum I Regem Romanorum*.[180] Ghent, Brescia, Florence, Naples, and the Vatican each possesses a single manuscript of this text—but *not one* of these five is based on the author's manuscript. The Ghent volume is a transcript on vellum of the edition printed at Alost by Thierry Martens shortly after the oration had been delivered (13 August 1486); the other four all derive from the Venetian edition produced by Antonius de Strata towards the end of August in that same year. One would have thought that these two editions, plus the Rome incunable issued by Stephan Plannck and the Nuremberg one of Peter Wagner, would have satisfied the demand and made it quite unnecessary to write out copies of what is, when all is said and done, a fairly ephemeral tract.

The close of the fifteenth century by no means brought an end to this practice of copying early printed books. For example, there is in my possession a manuscript of the *De origine mundi* by Alcimus Avitus, Bishop of Vienne (who died early in the sixth century), with a colophon which states that the volume was transcribed, from the first printed edition (of 29 August 1507), by Brother Walter Johannis on Saturday, 29 November 1522. A much more ambitious undertaking was the copying (1582-1590) of a *Missal* printed by Christopher Plantin in Antwerp, 1571, to which some five hundred illustrations were added.[181] From the seventeenth century, too, examples of such transcriptions can be cited. Thus, I own a manuscript of the *Dictes and Sayings of the Philosophers* which has the subscription: "Wrytten oute for mee by my man John May in May 1621," apparently at the instance of Sir Peter Manwood.[182] Antiquarianism[183] is probably the correct explanation for the preparation of this copy. By the eighteenth century, calligraphers had also seized upon early printed books as suitable models for their use. Mr. Philip Hofer owns a fascinating manuscript of the comedy of "Il Filosofo" by Pietro Aretino, written in North Italy in 1762 by the calligrapher Amadeo Mazzoli of Friuli.[184] This is an almost perfect facsimile of the 1546 Venetian edition of this text. Though it would in no way diminish the value of this manuscript as a remarkable example of calligraphic skill, it would have been a curious

36

twist of fate if the artist had chosen for his purpose, instead
of the genuine Giolito edition, a copy of the forgery turned out
at Brescia by Faustino Avogadro in 1730.

At first glance it would seem as though such manuscript
transcripts of printed books[185] would be worthless in the extreme—but, fortunately, this is not the case. Oddly enough,
a number of them are of high value for the study of scribal
habits and practices. When the immediate prototype is a
printed edition, then an absolute control is available for judging
the work of a scribe. It happens but rarely, in the case of manuscripts copied from manuscripts, that the precise "Vorlage" [186]
of a copy can be determined beyond question, so that it is
impossible, as a result, to judge how faithful or how inaccurate
a scribe may be—or even can be, when he so wishes—in
regard to his source. But when one can lay an incunabulum
side-by-side with its manuscript copy, then the scribe's capabili-
ties or lack of them, his mannerisms and personality, quickly
become apparent. Erasmus Stratter, for example, copied the
Mentelin German Bible of *circa* 1466 into a manuscript which
is now in the Graz University Library, but in doing so, he
altered the original dialect into his own Austro-Bavarian
tongue.[187] Here, Stratter was taking no more liberties than
did Diebold Lauber who, in supplying his customers with
manuscripts of the "höfische Epik" freely modernized the
texts.[188] Harley MS. 6149 is a copy of Caxton's *Order of
Chivalry,* but the dialect in the codex is no longer that of
London.[189] The text of the manuscript is thoroughly Scottish,
and there are other examples of such transformation. In the
Newberry Library, there is a text of the *Dictes and Sayings of
the Philosophers.*[190] Though this was obviously copied from
Caxton's first printing, it is a somewhat shortened version and

37

the dialect is clearly neither that of the author (Earl Rivers) nor that of the printer. In this case, the scribe may have improved on the English style of his original—the sentences seem better and more pithy—but he was not a faithful copyist. In Morgan MS. 801 there is a transcription of the Ratdolt edition (Venice: 1481) of the *Fasciculus temporum* of Werner Rolewinck.[191] In several places, the scribe obviously did not understand the meaning of the text and the method of its composition, so that there the copy offers the reader a totally incomprehensible mess.

Even more valuable than the evidence which such manuscripts produce for the scribal habits and traditions of the day are the instances where the manuscripts are the sole evidence that such editions ever existed. In a "Sammelband" of the Yale University Library,[192] there is a copy of the *Carmen Sapphicum* of Pope Pius II with a colophon: "Impressum est in Augusta per Gintherum Zainer de Reutlingenn"—but no Zainer edition of this text has come to light. A Vienna manuscript is a copy of the *Hortulus animae* printed by Martin Flach in Strassburg in 1510,[193] but again no copy of the original seems to have survived. In my own library, there is a late sixteenth-century manuscript of the *Life of St. Winifrid* which has the note that it was: "Drawen out of an ould pryntinge booke word by word." It is not quite certain precisely what meaning the word "printing" may have here, whether the prototype was printed from movable type or was the result of hand-lettering. Though the text is based on Caxton's account in the *Golden Legend,* it differs notably from this. I have not yet succeeded in finding the printed edition, if there ever was one, from which this manuscript was copied.[194] MS. Douce 261 of the Bodleian Library is a 1564 copy of an early print of the *The Jeaste of Syr Gawayne*,[195] but again I have been unable to locate the source. The value of these manuscripts, where the printed originals have completely disappeared, is quite self-evident.

We have seen how the scribe met the competition of the press, adjusting to it in a variety of ways. In the preface to his edition of the *Letters* of St. Jerome, which Conrad Sweynheym and Arnoldus Pannartz printed at Rome in 1468,[196] Johannes Andreae, the Bishop of Aleria, asserted that the most desirable books could henceforth be purchased for what blank paper and unused vellum formerly fetched—and that books were now priced for what one had once been wont to pay for a binding. Furthermore, these volumes were correctly "written," not most erroneously made, as the work of the scribes is characterized. It is ironic to think that the scribe Theodericus Nycolaus Werken de Abbenbroeck solemnly transcribed this statement into the manuscript of the *Epistolae* which he copied out in 1477 and which is now MS. R. 17. 4 in the library of Trinity College, Cambridge.[197]

II
THE PRINTERS

A VOLUME in the British Museum, which contains the text of Boccaccio's prose romance *Il
Filocolo*, has this note at the end: "Magister
Johannes[1] Petri de Magontia scripsit hoc opus
Florentiae." To this is added a Latin date which corresponds
to our 12 November 1472. A companion volume in the same
library, with the *Trionfi* by Petrarch, has a comparable colophon; this reads in translation: "Master Hans Petri of Mainz
wrote this work on February 22nd," the year having apparently
been forgotten, in any case it is omitted.[2] Though, as is well
known, many manuscripts written even in the first half of the
fifteenth century were provided with signature marks, foliation
or pagination, catch-words, headlines, and other such guides,
neither that Boccaccio nor the Petrarch which we have just
described has these refinements. What—one may well ask—
is so significant about this? Hundreds of manuscripts were
signed and dated by the scribes who wrote them; an even
larger number of them, written in the second half of this
same century, were not provided with these technical aids for
the assembling of the leaves nor with the handy means for
easy reference to specific sections of text, which were mentioned
just now. The significant thing here is that these volumes are
not manuscripts at all; they are, beyond possible question,
printed books. This again emphasizes the fact, already presented
in the first lecture, that the fifteenth century itself made little
distinction between hand-written and press-printed books.[3]
Indeed, in their own day, the early printed books were some-

40

times called by the curious term "codices . . . absque calami ulla exaracione effigiati" [4] and as volumes "escriptz en lettre d'impression," to distinguish them from those that were "escriptz à la main." [5] Francesco Filelfo, in a letter of 25 July 1470, expressed his interest in acquiring some of those new books produced by types which, he said, "seem to be the work of a skilled and exact scribe." [6] One cannot deal with the early years of printing without casting an occasional—or better, a continuing—glance at the tradition, habits, and methods of the scribes, as will be made evident later. [7]

The invention of the press came at a time exactly suitable for its advent. [8] The use of paper for the production of manuscript volumes had become increasingly frequent in the first half of our century. It may also be remarked that plenty of it seems to have been available when the press first began to operate, for the increase in paper-making facilities was one of the significant economic results of the Council of Basel (1431-1449). [9] The reading public had thereby become accustomed to a physical material suitable for books which was at once cheaper [10] than vellum and whose source of supply was not dependent upon the whims of Mother Nature. Paper production could be increased rapidly (the production of calves could not)— and it is clear that the growth of the number and size of paper-mills, in the decades after 1450, must have been quite phenomenal. That paper volumes, in turn, were regarded as "cheap and nasty" is suggested by a ruling promulgated at Cambridge in 1480, which stipulated that books on paper could not qualify as a pledge for loans. [11] Vellum volumes, however, continued to be acceptable, and they were the most commonly used guarantee for such purposes. [12] So far as books on vellum are concerned, one wonders how the suddenly increased demand for the raw material was met in a practical way by the purveyors. Allowing for the normal requirements of the scribes, assessed over many years and probably quite constant in view of the continuing demand for books in the face of an equivalent shortage of them prior to 1450, it is plain that the "parchmenters" were, all of a sudden and quite unexpectedly, faced by the needs of the press for hundreds and hundreds of skins for which they were completely unprepared. In the case of the 42-line (Gutenberg) Bible, it has been computed [13] that each copy required 170 calf-skins, with the result that the thirty odd copies believed to have been produced "sur vélin" used up the skins of no less than 5,000 calves, at a cost of some 335 gulden. Nor did much time elapse—if there was any lapse whatsoever—before thousands of additional skins were needed for the several score of copies of the 1457 and 1459 Psalters, the *Canon Missae*, the Durandus, the *Constitutiones* of Pope Clement V, the *Catholicon* (all sizable books),[14] and the other smaller publications on vellum issued prior to 1461.[15] All this vellum was not only required, it was obviously made available to the printer apparently without trouble;[16] and this need was satisfied, it should be borne in mind, on top of the normal demand (as in previous years) with which the press in no way interfered. Where this enormous quantity of vellum came from is none of our concern, since this is a problem in economic history—but it does give one pause to think! In the continental butcher-shops of the 1450s, there must have been a continuous "special" on Kalbskeule, scaloppine, and tête-de-veau!

The other condition which facilitated the rapid development and spread of the art and craft of printing was the very considerable extent of literacy to be found everywhere through-

out the civilized Europe of that day.[17] The size of the literate
public in the fifteenth century has been a matter of differing
opinions for many years[18]—and it seems unlikely that an
accurate appraisal, or sufficient proof for a sound estimate, will
ever be forthcoming. But such evidence as there is at our dis-
posal would justify the conclusion that the proportion of the
fifteenth-century populace that could read and write was much
greater than is usually supposed.[19] It is certain that, since the
thirteenth century, laymen could write—and merchants, of
course, *had* to be able to do so. In England, certainly, the
Pastons, the Stonors, the Plumptons, the Celys, and their
friends, could all read and write with ease[20]—and the same
must surely have been true of the Fuggers, the Medici, and the
Jacques Coeurs of the continent. We know of posters pro-
claiming matters of general interest that were affixed in public
places; why was this done, if no one could read them? [21] We
have examples of handwriting by uneducated persons[22]—and
being uneducated, it should be remembered, is not the same
as being illiterate, not by a long chalk. In England, in 1489,
the rules governing the "benefit of clergy" were changed, quite
obviously because the literate public had grown so large that
it was taking excessive advantage of this "benefit," with the
result that the "ground rules" needed changing.[23] If one adopts
Sir Thomas More's estimate of 1523,[24] one must then conclude
that half the population of fifteenth-century England could
read. It was the considered opinion of a great scholar[25] of our
own times that, in the century of our concern, "no person of
any rank or station in society above mere labouring men seems
to have been wholly illiterate. All could write letters: most
persons could express themselves in writing with ease and
fluency." Thus when Gutenberg made his invention, assuming

43

for the nonce that Johann Gensfleisch was indeed the inventor of this art,[26] both an adequate reading public and an economical vehicle suitable for use in the mechanically produced book were at hand.

Once the press was firmly established, there came the problem of its effect on the confraternity of scribes. Ultimately, as it is quite apparent to us, the hand-written book, and subsequently also the hand-written document, lost the battle with the press and withdrew from the field—but in the fifteenth century, it has been stressed, there was sufficient room for *both* the scribes and the printers.[27] In those years, the manuscript continued to be produced on *private* commission and needed to satisfy only the one person who had ordered it. Printing, on the other hand, was a *public* venture, the success of which depended entirely on the reception of its productions by a large and varied clientele. Every man, as we have seen, could be his own scribe, but every man could *not* become his own printer.

The relations between the scribe and the printer varied, naturally, from place to place—but if a general statement be permitted, it is that the scriveners as a whole did not immediately enter into pitched battle with the new craft of printing. In some cities, as was only to be expected, there was strong opposition to the press. At Genoa, on 11 May 1472, the scribes appealed to the Signoria against the printers,[28] especially to the effect that they should be prevented from issuing a variety of service books and common school-texts, books for which there was a ready market everywhere and for which the scribes, consequently, wished to secure preemptive rights. The complaint of the Augsburg Formschneider, Briefmaler, and Kartenmacher against Günther Zainer and Johann

Schüssler is, I am sure, familiar to every student of proto-typography.[29] In Paris, the Sorbonne demanded the total suppression of the press as late as 1533. This was, it is quite true, granted by François Premier in the following year—but, fortunately, the edict never took effect since it was not registered with Parliament.[30]

In Bologna[31] and Naples,[32] on the other hand, scribes seem to have been willing, even anxious, to assist the budding industry. At Hagenau[33] and Blaubeuren,[34] towns of modest size and with a correspondingly small market for books, scribes and printers lived in peace and harmony, so far as we know. In the flourishing Hanseatic city of Lübeck,[35] it was possible for Steffen Arndes, at the turn of the century, to be at once a Gerichtsschreiber and a printer.[36] Jacob Köbel, in the early years of the next, found no difficulty in being both a printer in and the Stadtschreiber of Oppenheim am Rhein,[37] while at Erfurt[38] the writing-master Johannes Brune, in 1493 to 1510, installed himself at the sign of The Pied Lion, where a press also appears to have been in operation during some of these years.

Since so much of the printing practices paralleled the activities of the scribes, it is not surprising that cooperation between the two sooner or later became inevitable. In practical ways, this can be seen in the printed *Canon Missae*,[39] which was produced about the year 1458 by Johann Fust and Peter Schoeffer, apparently for the express purpose of being inserted into manuscripts. That scribes sometimes used printed sections to simplify their own task may well explain Lambeth MS 7,[40] an Antiphoner in which the Calendar is a printed gathering. Conversely, there are many examples of early printed books which have leaves supplied in contemporary manuscript.[41] Presumably, when it was discovered that insufficient sheets had been run off to complete the copies on hand,[42] the printer was either obliged to reprint the wanting leaves or, if only a few were needed, to have a scribe write out the text, the manuscript leaves being bound up with the printed ones. If there were lacunae[43] which did not come to light until the unbound copies had reached the binder, then he had no alternative except to seek the assistance of the scribes in order to perfect the volumes.

The traditions of the hand-written book were often minutely followed by the pressman.[44] Not long ago I showed how the format of law books printed in Bologna corresponded closely to the university regulations laid down for the "pecia," although the press was not bound by these same rules.[45] Production problems were materially lessened for the printer when he adopted the principles of lay-out, the rules for the appearance of the printed word in line and page, which had long been standard practice for the calligraphers.[46] It is not improbable that calligraphers were hired to supervise this aspect of the printer's profession. In any case, it was natural for the printer to follow the models supplied to him by the scribe, particularly since many scribes not only became printers in the long run, but also assisted the press, from time to time, when their special talents were needed. It is self-evident that, in the design of his letters, the printer could turn *only* to the calligrapher. The study of scribal hands, then,[47] is of immense importance for the expert knowledge of early types. It has even been suggested that calligraphers, in turn, copied types, with particular reference to those of Nicolaus Jenson.[48] His founts, it is argued, found favor throughout Italy, and the copyists are supposed to have vied in imitating them to the greatest extent possible. But it has been strenuously denied, by the opposing school of thought concerned with the history of the written word, that such a happening ever took place. In the final analysis, the press amply repaid the calligraphers for their services by publishing calligraphic manuals for the schooling and use of the practitioners of this craft.[49]

To cite another example—perhaps not so familiar—of scribal usage taken over by the printer, one may recall the tendency for a manuscript to become "a leisurely accumulation of heterogeneous texts." [50] This resulted from the fact that, whenever blank pages were at hand, the scribe would fill these with odd, short texts, whether related to the other material or not.[51] William Caxton gladly adopted this practice, so that at the end of his *Court of Sapience* we find a conglomeration of prose texts (including one on the Decalogue, lists of virtues and vices, and the like) which have no visible connection with the anonymous poem that occupies thirty-six of the forty leaves.[52] At the conclusion of his edition of Lydgate's *Horse, Sheep, and Goose,* faced with five blank pages to follow, Caxton elected to use four of them to print a motley collection of information, which William Blades has described as: "The Proper Use of Various Nouns Substantive and Verbs." A great many such examples could be cited.[53]

Scribes also acted as editors for the printers. We find Giovan Marco "Cinico" da Parma (1430?-1497?) performing in this capacity for Mathias Moravus of Naples, at the same time writing many fine manuscripts.[54] The same press could also rejoice in the services of Pietro Molino, a "valente calligrafo" (1475-1508) [55] who was also the "custos" of the Biblioteca Aragonese. As the British Museum's incunabula catalogue points out,[56] it was the skill of the Dominican nuns of S.

Jacopo di Ripoli in Florence which, in all probability, suggested to their conventual procurator, Fra Domenico da Pistoia, and to their confessor, Fra Piero da Pisa, that a press might fittingly be established in the convent in the Via della Scala.

In the first half-century of printing, countless scribes, from Peter Schoeffer[57] to Antoine Vérard,[58] forsook the careers for which they had been trained in order to try their success with the new "artium omnium magistra." Some of them, like Arnaldus de Bruxella at Naples,[59] Colard Mansion in Bruges,[60] and Johann Schüssler of Augsburg,[61] became discouraged, gave up the press, and resumed their former rôles as scribes. The same situation may have prevailed in the case of Johann Bämler also of 'Augsburg,[62] who had been a scribe and subsequently took up printing, working at the press from 1477 to 1495; thereafter we know nothing of his career, though he continued on the tax list, presumably as a "Schreiber," until 1508.[63]

It is very difficult to discover what sort of individuals were tempted to try their luck with the new profession.[64] Professional scribes were probably raised to their craft from earliest youth and need never have had any other (or earlier) career. But, in the infancy of printing, each printer to be had to forsake some trade, profitable or otherwise, to embark on a venturesome and unpredictable future. Unfortunately, relatively few personal records are available to us in regard to the men who risked their all in this trade. We have absolutely no information in regard to eighty-eight of the 187 printers who figure in Ernst Voulliéme's *Die deutschen Drucker des fünfzehnten Jahrhunderts* (Berlin, 1922). Of the ninety-nine others, as I have counted them, thirty-six had university careers behind them; twenty-two were artists, including six Formschneider; fifteen belonged to the patrician classes; thirteen had been scribes;[65] eleven were in holy orders, and a similar number had been booksellers (including two former dealers in manuscripts).[66] Of course, among the later fifteenth-century printers, some had never had any other profession, having been raised directly into this trade. Such a man was Johann Froben of Hammelburg in Franconia, the distinguished scholar-printer of Basel, who later became Erasmus's publisher and the celebrated host at the Froben house "Zum Kessel." [67] He had begun life as a "famulus" in the firm of Johann Amerbach, another master-printer who had studied at the University of Paris. But a delightfully variegated background comes to light when we study the biographies of the early printers; in Germany, these range from a University Rector (Andreas Frisner, printer at Leipzig and Nuremberg) [68] and a monk [69] (Heinrich Wirtz-burg[70] from Vach near Nuremberg) all the way to a publican[71] and a barber-surgeon (respectively, Konrad Kachelofen of Leipzig, and Hans Folz of Nuremberg).[72] Artists, too,[73] embraced the new profession, including the Dombaumeister, Matthaeus Roritzer of Regensburg, and Bernardus Cenninus,[74] the "aurifex omnium judicio praestantissimus," as the Italian unashamedly describes himself, who had helped Ghiberti in the completion of one of the doors for the Florentine Baptistery and had also executed reliefs for the silver altar of St. John the Baptist in the same edifice.[75] A versatile man was Damianus de Moyllis of Parma who, though a "miniator et stampator a libris," dabbled in ceramics, binding, and calligraphy, printed a *Chorale* in 1477 along with a few other books, and produced numerous liturgical manuscripts; in his spare moments, he was a bookseller and wrote a calligraphic manual on lettering.[76]

"Haec sancta, ars," as Cusanus[77] was pleased to call it, certainly attracted to itself a splendid variety of men—and at least one woman, a widow by the name of Anna Rügerin, a resident of Augsburg. It may be proper to inquire next as to what the scholars of the day thought of the efforts of these printers.[78] Their opinion was equally varied; they viewed Gutenberg's invention either as a blessing or as a curse— sometimes both, at the same time.[79] Georgius Merula, for example, was quite uncertain which it was.[80] Among those who were vocal in their denunciation of bad printing was Francesco dal Pozzo, the Bolognese humanist who had himself been a partner in a printing firm.[81] In the preface to his edition of Tacitus, he complained of how the Venetian printers had mixed up and disfigured "this divine work" and that it was scarcely possible to make any sense out of it.[82] Francesco Filelfo,[83] writing to Cardinal Marco Barbo on 16 February 1476, complained of the Roman printers who had so corrupted parts of his *De Jesu Christi sacerdotio* that it was incomprehensible. A little over a year later, in a letter to Bernardo Giustiniano of 7 April 1477, he found similar fault with the Milanese craftsmen, in connection with his translation of Xenophon's *Cyropaedia*.

The printers, naturally, countered such criticism as best they could. While Benedictus Hectoris of Bologna laid the blame for faulty texts squarely on scribe and printer alike ("vitio scriptorum et impressorum incuria"),[84] Plato de Benedictis of the same city disclaimed all responsibility, maintaining that all faults were due to "the carelessness of his associates." [85] Aldus Manutius, the master-printer of Venice, pointed out the difficulties of providing a pure text. It was hard, he allowed, to produce a good Latin text, harder still a correct Greek one, and, hardest of all, a text free from errors.[86] Caxton, more

humbly, suggested to "theym that shal fynde faute to correcte
it & in so doyng they shal deserue thankynges & I shal praye
god for them." [87] Bernardo Cennini, the Florentine artist noted
earlier, in his edition of the commentary on Vergil by Servius,
boasted that his son Pietro, "as you may discover, has emended
[the text] with all the care and diligence of which he was
capable. Nothing [he adds] is difficult for Florentine genius." [88]
The correctness of the text is stressed in many colophons of
the period, even as the copyists had done—and sometimes
with just as little justification. [89] But the attitude of superiority
adopted by some printers vis-à-vis the scribes may have been
a defensive reaction to the implication that the new art was
mechanical and inferior—and, consequently, somehow baser
than the art of writing. [90] For those who wish to consult a
contemporary evaluation of the "pros" and "cons" in regard to
the press, there is Hieronymus Squarciafico's most curious composition in the form of a letter, dated 23 November 1481, sent
to him from the Elysian Fields by Francesco Filelfo, who had
died the previous 31st of July. [91]

Whatever it may have been that persuaded a worthy citizen
to seek his fortune with the press and whatever the opinions
may have been as to the results of his endeavors, one thing is
certain: the venture required a whole lot of capital. [92] You will
recall that it was Johann Fust's claim [93] that he had put over
2,000 gulden into Gutenberg's printing business—and even if
only the 1,600 be admitted which Gutenberg did not contest
—this was indeed a very large sum of money for those days.
The annual salary of the Stadtkanzler of Mainz, Dr. Konrad
Humery, [94] amounted to only 130 gulden in 1444, rising to 208
some years later; we have evidence to show that this latter figure
permitted him to live very handsomely. The sum which Fust

had been willing to risk in this business amounted, therefore, to at least the equivalent of ten years wages for a high-living city politician. In the Imperial city of Augsburg, in 1467, there were only sixty-three individuals with a taxable capital of 2,400 gulden, among the 4,510 citizens who were then on the tax-rolls.[95]

At this point, I should like to digress for a while upon a subject which deals with a matter of the greatest significance for the prototypographica. Some day, Deo volente, I should like to return to this problem in greater detail.

If, as seems likely, Fust was Gutenberg's sole "angel" and the inventor had no means of his own to put into the business, then the total investment in the printing plant was—at Fust's own estimate—just over 2,000 gulden. Now this sum must have sufficed to build six presses, since we are assured that the printing of the 42-line Bible proceeded simultaneously on that many.[96] This was the very first printing equipment to have been erected in Europe, and it can be assumed, I suppose, that these presses were more expensive than any similar ones built to the same design within the next few decades. The contemporary Wilhelm Wittwer,[97] in his account of the Abbots of SS. Ulrich and Afra in Augsburg, affirms that it cost the monastery seven hundred gulden to establish its printing plant in 1472. According to an official account of that year, Sixtus Saurloch provided two presses, with all the necessary appurtenances, at the request of Abbot Melchior von Stamheim, for the sum of 165 gulden.[98] When Johann Schüssler retired from printing, some time after he had completed the last book of which we have any record (6 March 1473),[99] he sold off his five used presses and their equally used accessories to the same monastery for the (perhaps bargain) price of 73 gulden.[100]

If we use the figure of 165 gulden for two presses, then each press could hardly have cost Gutenberg (twenty years earlier) much less than a hundred, for a total sum close to six hundred gulden. We have already seen that the price of the vellum[101] may well have been 335 gulden or more, based on an estimate of thirty such copies, though a total of thirty-five vellum copies has also been envisaged, at a corresponding cost for the hides of 390 gulden.[102] The paper for five times as many ordinary copies as vellum ones could hardly have cost any less; indeed, Schwenke[103] figures the expense for the paper at nine hundred gulden. This affords an approximate average estimate of 1,500 gulden for the bare essentials expended upon the press, and this would have left Gutenberg with an unexpended capital of anywhere from one hundred to 520 gulden.[104] Six presses are utterly useless, however, unless one has the man-power to operate them, and at least two men were needed to work each of them.[105] To this total, one must add the personnel required to set and distribute the type, to attend to the necessary proof-reading, and to make stop-press and other corrections—certainly not less than one man to every two presses, more logically one for each. With Gutenberg himself as the general manager, expert mechanic, and all-around trouble-shooter, there must have been a minimum of sixteen men on Gutenberg's payroll [106]— perhaps as many as twenty or more. It has also been estimated that it took no less than two years to complete the printing of the Bible.[107] The money that Gutenberg had on hand, then, was enough to pay each employee (at the most liberal estimate) thirteen gulden per year—and, at the worst, less than two and a half gulden annually. For comparison's sake, we may note that a butchered calf, at Augsburg and in 1482, brought one gulden.[108] A copy of the *Catholicon* of 1460 cost forty-one gulden in 1465, while in 1474 the *Speculum historiale* of Vincent of Beauvais from the press of SS. Ulrich and Afra was sold for a price varying between twenty and twenty-four gulden.[109] It is also worthy of our consideration that Dr. Humery's salary[110] would, under these circumstances, have been sixty-five times that of a highly skilled craftsman, even if we make no allowance at all for whatever Gutenberg saw fit to pay himself or for the possibility that he might have had other expenses, such as those for rent,[111] coal, types, ink, and minor repairs. Does all this seem credible—or is there something fishy about our accepted beliefs and theories? Finally, if one subscribes to Paul Schwenke's figure[112] of 1,400 gulden for vellum and paper alone, then—after the building of the presses—there was no money whatever left over with which to pay the workmen. They may have been dedicated to "this holy art"—but they could hardly have afforded to be that dedicated for two whole years!

Though a relatively large investment was required by the press, this did not seem to deter anyone from embarking on a publishing career. The early printer, of course, was an active entrepreneur in this field of activity, too, in addition to the purely mechanical duties of his profession. On balance, very few of those who pioneered in this field made a success of it;[113] they were lucky when they could make a bare living from it, the result (quite obviously) of the ruinous competition between the presses which arose almost immediately in every city into which the new art penetrated. The law of supply and demand operated as well (or as unhappily, according to one's point of view) in the fifteenth century as it does today. In Venice,[114] some 150 separate printing offices hopefully opened their doors within thirty-one years, an average of nearly five firms a year from 1469 to 1501; this list does *not* include a substantial number of anonymous establishments. Of this total, a mere handful made a real success of their undertaking, judging from the length of time they continued to operate and what little, unfortunately, we know of their financial status when the printers finally had to close their books. Certainly, the Schoeffers, the Quentells, the Silbers (alias Francks), the Manuzii, the Crombergers (on both sides of the Atlantic), and other such families maintained a successful business over generations—and there were individuals, also, who enjoyed large financial rewards from their endeavors, such as Günther Zainer, Anton Koberger,[115] Antoine Vérard, Stephan Plannck, and so on. Zainer, as we have already remarked, was one of Augsburg's wealthiest citizens in his day, being one of the sixty-three who paid the highest taxes. Erhard Ratdolt, in 1498, appears as number 117, of the 5,050 names on the tax-rolls; he was one of the 143 Augsburgers whose capital exceeded 2,400 florins.[116] When William Caxton died, the charges for his funeral were considerably higher than those for most of his fellow-parishioners at St. Margaret's in Westminster, indicating that he was a man of outstanding eminence in his community. That Caxton's means were more than just adequate may be judged from the fact that Gerard Crop claimed that he had been willed £80 by the printer, his father-in-law.[117] Apparently, this formed part of a nuncupative will, since there is no record of any such provision other than Crop's statement; a will of this sort was legally valid until the reign of Charles II. The press, then, was capable of creating a whole new class of wealth, something which copying by itself could never achieve. As a general statement, it may be remarked that the press fared

55

better in the big commercial metropolises (Milan, Venice, Basel, Strassburg, and London—or rather its neighbouring Westminster)[118] than in university centers, such as Heidelberg and Oxford, or in episcopal cities, if Orleans and Narbonne, Eichstädt and Meissen, Gerona and Murcia may be cited. Then it probably also is true that native citizens, like Koberger, Ratdolt, and Caxton, had a considerable advantage over the "foreigners," at least in getting along with the local guilds.

But these successes were the exceptions! The potential output, a practically unlimited one made possible by the new mechanical means,[119] almost immediately fostered the bitterest sort of competition. A flood of books suddenly hit a market where shortages had previously been the chronic complaint.[120] It has been estimated that Günther Zainer[121] alone printed some 36,000 books at a time when the entire population of Augsburg amounted to only half that number.[122] In 1471 to 1473 a series of crises in the book industry shook the Italian peninsula. The market was glutted with unsold books.[123] Quite similar to the present-day cycle of boom and bust, these disasters seem to have taught no one a lesson, then any more than now. By 1500, the market was once again saturated. In 1503, Koberger wrote to Johann Amerbach, his associate in Basel, that the clergy was now book-poor: "man hatt die pfaffen So gancz aussgelertt mitt den buchern, so vil gelcz von jn czogen, Das [sie] nicht mer dar an wollen." [124] No fewer than six of the fifteen earliest Basel printers went broke; probably the number would be even higher if we had full biographical details on all the members of the guild.[125] The roll of the names of those Germans[126] who, sooner or later, suffered serious financial setbacks or finally had to admit total defeat reads like the roster of the typographers' Hall of Fame: Johann Gutenberg; Johann Neumeister, unsuccessful in three countries; Ulrich Zell, the first printer in Cologne; Johann Zainer, Konrad Dinckmut, and Lienhart Holle, the first three printers in Ulm; and all of the Brandis boys of Lübeck and Leipzig (Matthew, Mark, Luke—I wish I could add: John).[127] On the other hand, Heinrich Molitor seems to have been one of the very few scribes who, we know for certain, died without wealth or property.[128]

Bitter competition and the threat of bankruptcy,[129] a dire proceeding in those days, probably provided the reasons which impelled so many printers to "hit the road," a situation somewhat paralleled by the travelling photographers of the nineteenth century. Men like Jacobinus Suigus (who worked successively in San Germano, Vercelli, Chivasso, Venice, Turin, and Lyons),[130] Henricus de Colonia (with presses in Bologna, Brescia, Lucca, Modena, Nozzano, Siena and Urbino, at various times),[131] and the Johann Neumeister[132] just referred to, are characteristic of this category. For a fascinating summary of the career of Johann Beckenhub, I heartily recommend Victor Scholderer's interesting account printed some years ago in *The Library*.[133]

A corollary to the problem of the peripatetic printer is that of the small town, which, in the fifteenth century, produced only a few books and is then heard of no more. Allied to this is the mysterious appearance of a well-known printer in some place where he produced only a single book. Does the colophon[134] in each case tell us the absolute truth—or did the printer deliberately insert a false statement into these books to attract possible purchasers? That is, could not such a book have been printed elsewhere for sale in the place called for in the colophon, the printer hoping that local pride might promote the sale of his goods? Occasionally there seems to be some strong evidence in favor of this assumption, as I have more fully set forth in my book on the Bolognese press.[135] Cicero's *De amicitia* was printed at Leipzig by Melchior Lotter with a colophon simply reading "Heidelberge impressus," where this printer is not known to have worked. The *Gesamtkatalog der Wiegendrucke* (no. 7001) argues that Lotter was reprinting a Heidelberg incunable which has not survived, but the Leipzig edition (possibly post-1500) is rather late for this sort of explanation to be thoroughly acceptable. I should think that it is not impossible that Lotter printed this book in Leipzig with a view to selling it in Heidelberg. The Albericus de Rosate (GW 529) is known with two colophons, one indicating Milan and the other Venice as the place of printing. Was the edition to be divided and a part put on sale in each city? But colophons so often give misleading information, either wilfully[136] (as in the case of piracies and forgeries,[137] or when the publisher—for one reason or another —wanted to deceive the purchaser)[138] or accidentally,[139] when a printer too faithfully followed his copy, that one cannot always interpret the facts satisfactorily. Consider the edition of the *Meditationes de interiori homine* wrongly ascribed to St. Bernard and described by the *Gesamtkatalog* under number 4033. The colophon states that the book was printed at Strassburg in 1492, and the contents, we are assured, were taken from the edition preceding this in the bibliography. But *neither* of these editions was printed in Strassburg! The earlier, which lists no place of origin, is now assigned to the press of Johann Amerbach at Basel; the later one was put out by Bernardinus Benalius in Venice. Had this printer simply assumed that his prototype came from Strassburg—and if so, why?

There is good evidence for the assumption that a certain amount of export business was carried on in the incunabula period.[140] A number of years ago, I pointed out that an edition of Petrarch's *Patient Griselda* in German, which was indubitably printed in Ulm about 1473 by Johann Zainer, was clearly designed for sale in Augsburg, since it was printed in the dialect used in that city and not in the one current in Ulm. Nor was this, in all probability, the only book so printed by Johann Zainer. Later in the century, Anton Koberger had books manufactured for him by Adolf Rusch in Strassburg[141] and by Johann Amerbach in Basel;[142] in the sixteenth century, he also made use of Adam Petri in that same city.[143]

In the hope of determining the sort of books which the first printers thought would sell well, I analyzed twenty-three booksellers' advertisements, all from German presses.[144] It seemed likely that the producers of the volumes would be glad to advertise those items which they believed to be most useful in attracting the interest of prospective purchasers. Furthermore, some of the items listed in the advertisements have, since then, totally disappeared; such works were practically always popular or profane works in the vernacular, which were quite literally "read to pieces" by avid readers. It seemed promising, therefore, that the advertising lists might supply a better statistical picture of what actually was put out than figures based only on surviving books.[145] I must confess, with regret, that the results obtained were hardly worth the effort expended on them. The advertisements listed 176 books in all, of which exactly a hundred (or 56.8%) were in Latin and the rest (or 43.2%) in German. Religious books predominated, with forty-four in Latin and twenty-four in German. Fifteen romances in German may, on the other hand, be contrasted with the five Bibles (three in Latin and two in German). Thirteen scientific works,[146] at least they were thought to be such in their own day, considerably outnumber those devoted to lives of the Saints (six in all).[147] But if anything very revealing can be gleaned from the figures given below, then it has quite evidently escaped my notice.

The books which appear in the advertisements may be listed in this fashion:

Bibles	5
Commentaries & Biblical texts	12
Bull	1
Didactic literature	10
Historical "	6
Legal "	11
Ancient " (with translations)	6
Mediaeval " " "	12
Liturgies (with Durandus)	4
Devotional and religious works	68
Romances	15
Saints' lives	6
Scientific works	13
Sermons	5
Travel books (German)	2
Total	176

In comparison with the printers' advertisements, the list offered by Diebold Lauber[148] for the manuscripts which he was prepared to supply[149] was a much "lighter" one. Although we are told that he spoke highly of his Latin books, only one work is specified as being in that tongue in the advertisement, and then only together with a German rendering: "ein Salter latin vnd tutsch." [150] It is evident that Lauber was prepared to supply his clientele—this being not the broad mass of the populace, as was once thought likely, but its upper crust— with instructive, entertaining, and useful books of all sorts, predominantly religious but with a good sprinkling of what the Germans solemnly call: "Unterhaltungsliteratur."

Sometimes it would seem that the choice of books selected for publication by the early presses was very unimaginative and stereotyped.[151] The Italian printers were all busily publishing the same classics, until many of them, as we have seen, became insolvent and had to close their doors. Four printers in Augsburg, a wealthy city but not by any means the largest in Germany, issued seven of the twelve High German Bibles produced in the fifteenth century[152]—and yet, apparently, it never occurred to one of the twenty-three presses that operated there in these years to print the Latin text. Conversely, five Basel firms turned out seventeen Latin Bibles, but not a single German one was issued by any of Basel's fifteen printing plants.[153] Although over thirty editions of the *De arte loquendi et tacendi* of Albertano da Brescia appeared before 1501, not one Italian press was sufficiently interested in this North Italian moralist and lawyer ("Causidicus" is the term), to risk putting the text into type, though the work found publishers in such diverse places as: Angoulême, Antwerp, Augsburg, Basel, Cologne, Deventer, Ingolstadt, Leipzig, Louvain, Lyons, Memmingen, Paris, Strassburg, and Toulouse.[154]

An impression has been created, mostly among the uninitiated, that a printed book is a somewhat inferior thing as compared with manuscripts, and that it was also considered so in its own day.[155] Repeatedly, we are treated to Vespasiano da Bisticci's remark that Federigo da Montefeltro's library was composed exclusively of manuscripts: "e non v'è ignuno a stampa" [156]—and that this was the general feeling towards printed books in the fifteenth century. Is this true? NOT AT ALL![157] One of the most celebrated of manuscript collectors, King Matthias Corvinus of Hungary, owned quite a number of incunabula[158]—and a number of manuscripts admittedly transcribed from them to boot, such as copies of the 1471 Curtius Rufus printed by Vindelinus de Spira in Venice[159] and of the 1470 St. Jerome produced at Rome by Sweynheym and Pannartz.[160] Corvinus also made use of the press and ordered the printing of the Esztergom Breviary and other liturgical volumes.[161]

Italian humanists were eager patrons of the press. Baptista da Guarino,[162] the son of the great Guarino da Verona, wrote to Pico della Mirandola from Ferrara on 5 December 1489 that "if possible, he would prefer to purchase printed editions of Capella and of Seneca's *Natural Questions.*" This, in turn, casts doubt on such a modern judgment as the one on Pico's own library, to the effect that: "The large proportion of the inventory labeled 'impressus' makes us regret less than we should otherwise the loss of this collection." [163] Pico had his choice, and he chose to buy printed versions; surely, he must have had excellent reasons for preferring them. Manifestly, "La Fenice degli Ingegni," as Ficino called him,[164] believed them to be more accurate than the manuscripts on the market —in which case, we must bitterly regret the loss of those editions which do not seem to have survived to our day. Of Francesco Filelfo's interest in incunabula we have already spoken, but his letter of 17 November 1470 to Johannes

Andreae may suitably be referred to here.[165] There he inquired from the Bishop of Aleria what was new in the world of printed books, presumably a matter of great curiosity to him which the Bishop, in his capacity as editor to Sweynheym and Pannartz, was in the position to satisfy. The Estes,[166] the Gonzagas, the Medici, King Ferdinand I of Naples[167]—such members of the nobility were quite willing to obtain examples of the new art. Even the Biblioteca Vaticana was not above admitting incunabula to its shelves as early as the fifteenth century.[168]

In Germany,[169] the situation was identically the same.[170] Hartmann Schedel, as we have seen, purchased printed books in Italy, and so did his fellow-townsman, Wilibald Pirckheimer. Celtes, Hutten, Wimpheling, Reuchlin—all became clients of the press.[171] Cardinal Nicolaus Cusanus's interest in printing is, of course, common knowledge. The monastery of Tegernsee bought incunabula by the hundreds,[172] and most Bavarian monasteries followed suit. At the secularization of these monastic institutions in 1803, the incunabula passed into the Bayerische Staatsbibliothek where they became both the basis for Ludwig Hain's great *Repertorium bibliographicum* and the great store-house of duplicates from which the book-trade could (and still does, I am told) replenish its stocks. Examples may be cited for France and England as well, naturally. The inventory of Bernard of Béarn, the Bastard of Comminges, of 1497, noted sixty-three books, practically all of which were printed.[173] John Shirwood, Bishop of Durham, bought chiefly printed books on his visits to Rome.[174] Though the Pastons, as typical landed gentry, owned relatively few books, they nevertheless counted incunabula amongst their possessions.[175] When Don Fernando Colón, the natural son of Christopher Columbus, visited London in June 1522, he was glad to purchase quite a number of fifteenth-century books, most of which, though printed on the continent, had been brought to England for sale.[176] In general, these were not the sort of books which would have appealed to "the man on the street." [177] Can one still pretend that printed books were scorned in their own day—or was the stigma of their inferiority due to the "snobisme" of such professional aristocrats as Federigo da Montefeltro? [178]

Matteo Battiferri[179] of Urbino studied medicine at Ferrara and thereafter practiced his profession in Venice. He was not just another general practitioner; as an "artium doctor et medicine," his interests were much broader than that. Battiferri was a poet; at any rate he wrote verse, however good or bad it may have been. He was also interested in the press and served as editor for the *Physica* of Albertus Magnus, issued from Venice by Johannes and Gregorius de Gregoriis, 8 January 1488 (Old Style), a work dedicated to his father, Jacobus. In addition, the good doctor found time to decorate his books, and he did a commendable job of illuminating his vellum copy of the *editio princeps* of the Greek Anthology[180] which is now, or in any event formerly was, in the Preussische Staatsbibliothek of Berlin. Battiferri, at the same time, made a slight alteration in the colophon where the printer, Laurentius Francisci de Alopa of Venice,[181] stated that the book had been printed in Florence on 11 August 1494. Doctor Matteo there expunged the word "impressum" and substituted "scriptum." On an extra leaf which he illuminated and inserted at the beginning of the volume, Battiferri stated (in Greek capitals) that he himself had written (ἐπιγράφω is the verb he chooses) and decorated it; by implication, one was expected to assume that this applied

AETHEREM.

ueit taurus sup ibribus austri
t tonitru crebraq. abscodit gradiē tras
ēperat i gemis annū nec crede sereno
ubila nec diuturna putes cū sidē cācri
onferit ardētis: tū hoc i littore certū
lagrātis placidae lucis hic temperat annū
ū posuit sedem. nemeis finibz astruz.

PLATE IIa
Aratus, *Phaenomena*
M 389, f. 77; written by Cinico
See pp. 27, 47, 129, 158
Collection: Morgan Library

PLATE IIb
Pietro Aretino, *Il Filosofo*
Manuscript, f. 1
See p. 36
Collection: Philip Hofer, Esq.

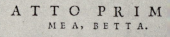

ATTO PRIM
MEA, BETTA.

	ONDE si uiene, d
	de o Betta?
Bet.	D'allogare una camer
	la Cencia, ch'è egli
	si uol dire; grauida
	me da il mondo.
Me.	Può essere?
Bet.	Cosi non fusse.
Me.	E pur ua a la predica, & digiuna,
Bet.	Ogni gatta ha il suo Gennaio, sorella.
Me.	Hora dimmi, come la fai tu cō le tue stāze a pig
Bet.	Me la trabatto cosi cosi. e pur hieri ne pigliò
	un compratore di belle pietre d'annella: che
	croce di Dio sta molto bene indaniato. e lo
	peroche a ogni parola ne sguaina fuora d
	manica un borsotto di quegli.
Me.	Guardi pure, che i mariuoli non glie ne attacch
Bet.	Gli è Perugino, non ti uuo dire altro; ha n
	Boccaccio, & è si tirato da i cani, che gua
	la gamba.
Me.	Di tu da senno?
Bet.	Dal miglior, ch'io habbi.
Me.	E dunque di la?
Bet.	Si dico.

annef Marcus uelox chryfo
olitanuf feruus natu
oyocos opinione maurus
apoli : trunglle tranferip

Sacro Busto, *Sphaera mundi* (Italian)
Colophon by Cinico (M 426)
(1) See *pp. 27, 47, 129, 158*
Collection: Morgan Library

Magifter iouannes petri demagontia feripfit hoc opus florêtiae
Die:XII:nouenbris:MCCCCLXXII:

Boccaccio, *Il Filocolo*
Florence: Petri, 12 Nov. 1472, colophon
(2) See *p. 40*
Collection: British Museum

mœdia hæc, cui titulus IL FILOSOFO . Au
re Petro Aretino, ab exemplari typis im
effo defumpta , transfcripta fuit a D.Ama
o Mazzoli Forojulienfi anno a partu Virgi
nis MDCCLXII.

Pietro Aretino, *Il Filosofo*
Colophon by Amadeo Mazzoli
(3) See *p. 36*
Collection: Philip Hofer, Esq.

PLATE IIIb
Psalter
Mainz: Fust & Schoeffer,
29 Aug. 1459, f. 1
See *p. 42*
Collection: Morgan Library

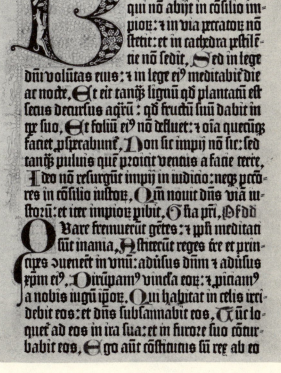

ay Herde of dere   a Byldyng of rokes
ay Herde of Swannys   a Clatering of chowghis
ay Herde of cranys   a Murmeracōn of stares
ay Herde of Wrennys   an Hoost of men
ay Herde of alle dere   an Hoost of sparowes
a Nepe of fesantes   a Felouship of ymen
a Couepe of partriches   a Gagyll of gees
a Beupe of larkes   a Gagyll of Women
a Beupe of ladyes   a Chyrme of fynches
a Beupe of quaylys   a Swarme of bees
a Beupe of roos   a Exaltacion of larkes
a Siege of byttours   a Discecion of Wodwales
a Siege of hyrons   a Mutacion
a Spryng of teeles   a Cety of greyes
a Sourd of malardes   ay Erthe of foxes
a Discete of lapwinkis   a Bery of conyes
a Muster of peocks   a Neste of rabettis
a Falle of Wodcocks   a Lytter of Whelpes
a Walke of snytes   a Reste of knyghtes
a Congregacōn of plouis   a Reste of Wolues
a Couerte of cootes   a Pryde of lyons
ay Snkmdnes of rauens   a Lepe of lebardes

PLATE IVa
Lydgate, *Horse, Sheep, and Goose*
[Westminster: Caxton, 1477], f. 16ᵛ
See p. 47
Collection: Morgan Library

Also fürt er sie auß dem hauß offenlich vnd zeiget sie al-
lermenig/die ist mein weib(sprach er)die ist ewer frow/
die söllen ir eren/die söllet ir lieb haben/vnd ob ir mich
lieb haben /so haben die für die aller türisten vñ besten

PLATE IVb
Petrarch, *Historia Griseldis* (German)
[Ulm: Zainer, 1473], f. 4
See p. 59
Collection: Morgan Library

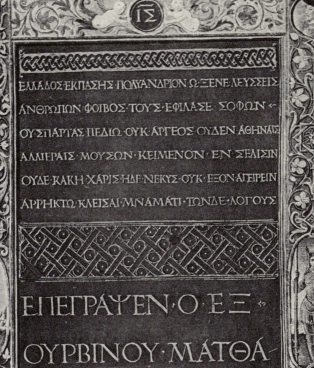

ΕΛΛΑΔΟΣ ΕΚΠΑΣΗΣ ΠΟΛΥΑΝΔΡΙΟΝ Ω ΞΕΝΕ ΛΕΥΣΣΕΙΣ
ΑΝΘΡΩΠΩΝ ΦΟΙΒΟΣ ΤΟΥΣ ΕΦΙΛΑΣΕ ΣΟΦΩΝ
ΟΥ ΣΠΑΡΤΑΣ ΠΕΔΙΩ ΟΥΚ ΑΡΓΕΟΣ ΟΥΔΕΝ ΑΘΗΝΑΙΣ
ΑΛΛ ΙΕΡΑΙΣ ΜΟΥΣΩΝ ΚΕΙΜΕΝΟΝ ΕΝ ΣΕΛΙΣΙΝ
ΟΥΔΕ ΚΑΚΗ ΧΑΡΙΣ ΗΔΕ ΝΕΚΥΣ ΟΥΚ ΕΞΟΝ ΑΓΕΙΡΕΙΝ
ΑΡΡΗΚΤΩ ΚΛΕΙΣΑΙ ΜΝΑΜΑΤΙ ΤΩΝΔΕ ΛΟΓΟΥΣ

ΕΠΕΓΡΑΨΕΝ Ο ΕΞ
ΟΥΡΒΙΝΟΥ ΜΑΤΘΑ
ΙΟΣ ΒΑΤΤΙΦΕΡΡΟΣ
ΙΑΤΡΟΣ ΟΣ ΚΑΙ
ΕΚΟΣΜΗΣΕΝ

PLATE V

Matteo Battiferri, illumination and script

(*Mittelalterliche Handschriften*, Leipzig, 1926, Tafel 8)

See p. 64

Collection: Berlin, Preuss. Staatsbibliothek

PLATE VIa
Rolewinck, *Fasciculus temporum*
M 801, f. 30
See p. 66
Collection: Morgan Library

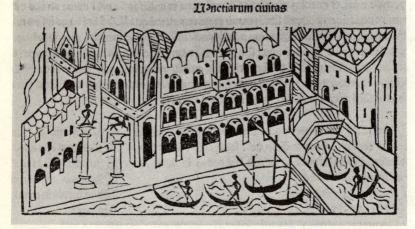

Uenetiarum ciuitas

PLATE VIb
Rolewinck, *Fasciculus temporum*
Venice: Ratdolt, 21 Dec. 1481, f. 37^v
See p. 66
Collection: Morgan Library

PLATE VII
Anthologia Graeca
Florence: Alopa, 11 Aug. 1494, f.
See p. 86
Collection: Morgan Library

ΑΡΧΙΟΥ. ΕΙΣ ΤΟΥΣ ΤΕΣΣΑΡΑΣ ΑΓΩΝΑΣ.

ΤΕΣΣΑΡΕΣ ΕΙΣΙΝ ΑΓΩΝΕΣ ΑΝ᾽ΕΛΛΑΔΑ. ΤΕΣ-
ΣΑΡΕΣ ΙΡΟΙ.
ΟΙ ΔΥΟ ΜΕΝ, ΘΝΗΤΩΝ. ΟΙ ΔΥΟ Δ᾽ΑΘΑ-
ΝΑΤΩΝ.
ΖΗΝΟΣ. ΛΗΤΟΙΔΑΟ. ΠΑΛΑΙΜΟΝΟΣ. ΑΡΧΕΜΟΡΟΙΟ.
ΑΘΛΑ ΔΕ ΤΩΝ, ΚΟΤΙΝΟΣ. ΜΗΛΑ. ΣΕΛΙΝΑ. ΠΙΤΥΣ.

ΔΙΟΤΙΜΟΥ. ΕΙΣ ΗΡΑΚΛΗΝ. ΚΑΙ ΑΝΤΑΙΟΝ.

ΤΑΝ ΗΒΑΝ ΕΣ ΑΕΘΛΑ ΠΑΛΑΣ ΗΣΚΗΣΕ ΚΡΑΤΑΙΑΣ
Α᾽ ΔΕ ΠΟΣΕΙΔΩΝΟΣ ΚΑΙ ΔΙΟΣ Α᾽ ΓΕΝΕΑ.
ΚΕΙΤΑΙ ΔΕ ΣΦΙΝ ΑΓΩΝ ΟΥ ΧΑΛΚΕΟΥ ΑΝΤΙ ΛΕΒΗΤΟΣ.
ΑΛΛ᾽ΟΣΤΙΣ ΖΩΑΝ ΟΙΣΕΤΑΙ Η ΘΑΝΑΤΟΝ.
ΑΝΤΑΙΟΥ ΤΟ ΠΤΩΜΑ, ΠΡΕΠΕΙ Δ᾽ΗΡΑΚΛΕΑ ΝΙΚΑΝ
ΤΟΝ ΔΙΟΣ. ΑΡΓΕΙΩΝ Α᾽ ΠΑΛΑ ΟΥ ΛΙΒΥΩΝ.

ΑΝΤΙΠΑΤΡΟΥ. ΕΙΣ ΑΡΙΑΝ.

Ο ΣΤΑΔΙΕΥΣ ΑΡΙΗΣ Ο ΜΕΝΕΚΛΕΟΣ, ΟΥ ΚΑΤΕΛΕΓΧΕΙ
ΠΕΡΣΕΑ ΣΟΝ ΚΤΙΣΤΗΝ, ΤΑΡΣΕ ΚΙΛΙΣΣΑ ΠΟΛΙ.
ΤΟΙΟΙ ΓΑΡ ΠΑΙΔΟΣ ΠΤΗΝΟΙ ΠΟΔΕΣ, ΟΥ Δ᾽ΑΝ ΕΚΕΙΝΩΣ
ΟΥ Δ᾽ΑΥΤΟΣ ΠΕΡΣΕΥΣ ΝΩΤΟΝ ΕΔΕΙΞΕ ΘΕΩΝ.
Η ΓΑΡ ΕΦ᾽ΥΣΠΛΗΓΓΩΝ, Η ΤΕΡΜΑΤΟΣ ΕΙΔΕ ΤΙΣ ΑΚΡΟΥ
ΗΙΘΕΟΝ. ΜΕΣΣΩΙ Δ᾽ ΟΥΠΟΤ᾽ΕΝΙ ΣΤΑΔΙΩΙ.

ΛΕΟΝΤΟΣ ΦΙΛΟΣΟΦΟΥ ΕΙΣ ΤΟ ΜΟΝΗΜΕΡΙΟΝ.

ΤΟΞΟΤΑ ΠΙΕΡΙΔΩΝ ΜΕΔΕΩΝ. ΕΚΑΤΗΒΟΛΕ ΦΟΙΒΕ.
ΕΙΠΕ ΚΑΣΙΓΝΗΤΗ· ΚΡΑΤΕΡΟΥΣ ΙΝΑ ΘΗ ΡΑΣ ΕΓΕΙΡΗ·
ΟΣΣΟΝ ΕΠΙΤΑΥΣΑΙ ΜΕΡΟΠΩΝ ΔΕΜΑΣ. ΟΣΣΟΝ ΑΥΣΑΙ
ΛΑΩΝ ΤΕΡΠΟΜΕΝΩΝ ΙΕΡΟΝ ΣΤΟΜΑ. ΜΗ ΔΕΝΟΗΣΩ   ΑΙΙ
ΖΗΝΟΣ ΜΕΙΛΙΧΙΟΙΟ ΛΑΧΩΝ ΘΡΟΝΟΝ ΑΝΕΡΟΣ ΟΙΤΟΝ.

not only to the inserted leaf but to the entire book. There still
were people, then, even in the closing years of the fifteenth
century, who wanted their "de luxe" volumes to be manuscripts
—or if not actually that, at least to *appear* to be manuscripts.

III
THE DECORATORS

N 1937, at the sale of the library of Lord Aldenham, the Pierpont Morgan Library acquired a manuscript which is now numbered 801 in the Library's collection.[1] According to the description of the volume supplied in 1914 by the celebrated palaeographer E. Maunde Thompson, then Keeper of Manuscripts in the British Museum, the first tract in the manuscript was a "Universal History (in Latin) on the plans of Martinus Polonus. 51 folios. MS. on paper, with 32 drawings." These illustrations—scenes of towns, landscapes, battles, and the like—are supplemented by a figure of a dolphin, a drawing of some "putti," and two border pieces. The work of the artist was executed with some care—and a good deal of trouble was taken with the embellishment of the book. Nevertheless, the artistic decoration of this manuscript is not an *original* contribution by some talented individual. All the drawings are direct copies of the woodcuts used in a printed volume—the entire work, in fact, being a verbatim hand-written reproduction of Erhard Ratdolt's edition of the *Fasciculus temporum* by Werner Rolewinck, printed at Venice in 1481.[2] The dolphin, the putti, and the borders, it is true, do not appear in the printed original, and some further decorative elements occur in the manuscript which are not to be found in the Ratdolt printing. It is not impossible, however, that these additional features may have been present as manuscript decoration in the particular copy which the scribe used as his exemplar.[3]

Also to be found in the Morgan Library is a copy of the

familiar *Speculum humanae salvationis* assigned to the press of
the "Printer of the Speculum"; this press is believed to have
been located at Utrecht, for a number of insufficient reasons
with which we need not concern ourselves.[4] The first "state,"
"issue," or whatever you may be pleased to call the earliest
printed appearance of this particular version consists of sixty-
four leaves; at the top of each page are woodcuts, below which
the text was printed by means of movable type. At some time
during the course of production of this work, something went
wrong with the printing. The obvious result was that there
were not enough impressions of certain leaves to make up the
number of copies which had originally been envisaged—and
the printer was thereupon obliged to make good this deficiency.
Such a situation is far from being an unusual occurrence among
early printed books[5]—but the present example is rather more
than uncommon by the very nature of the expedient for solving
his problem which the printer chose to use. Instead of setting
up the type afresh and running off the needed number of
copies, the printer had the required body of text cut as wood-
blocks and printed from these.[6] Why he did this—which seems
to us so primitive, cumbersome, and impractical a method—is
not at all clear. I have heard and read a variety of explanations,
but not one of them is very convincing. Nor is this use of a
woodblock under such circumstances a solitary example. The
popular elementary grammar by Aelius Donatus appeared in
well over 350 incunabula editions, but this did not deter publishers from issuing numerous printings of this text in which
the printed impression was produced from blocks cut in imitation of type-printed volumes.[7] Two issues of the *Forma con-
fessionalis*, an indulgence issued for the benefit of those con-
tributing to the war against the Turks in 1482, are xylographic

67

copies of the edition put out by Friedrich Creussner in Nuremberg.[8] At Westminster, William Caxton had issued quite a
number of books printed from movable type before he published his *Image of Pity,* with a "xylographic inscription imitating exactly [his] type 5." [9] On title-pages,[10] xylography
flourished along with typography well beyond the magic date of
1501.[11] Even an occasional blockbook of the sixteenth century
can be cited, such as the strange and remarkable *Opera nova
contemplativa* by Giovanni Andrea Vavassore apparently produced in Venice in the first quarter of the Cinquecento.[12]

The examples just enumerated are not haphazard citations.
They once again underline the evident fact, mentioned in the
previous lectures, that it was quite immaterial to the fifteenth-
century owner how his books were produced or decorated,
whether manually or mechanically.[13] The artist could copy the
woodcutter[14]—and the scribes and the woodcutters could
imitate the printers, or vice versa[15]—and it was all the same to
the contemporary purchaser. The fifteenth-century book, then,
cannot logically or properly be segregated into those neat
categories so dear to the heart of Library Schools: the autono-
mous departments of manuscripts and printed books. It is with
genuine satisfaction that one observes that the Austrian National Library has placed the incunabula in the keeping of the
"Direktor der Handschriftenabteilung."

At this point I should, perhaps, apologize to those who may
have been misled by the title of this chapter. I am not an art
historian, and broad color-blindness prevents me from ex-
pressing (publicly in any case) my views on the aesthetics of
the painted image. There are hundreds of excellent books on
manuscript illumination (we have a reading room full of them
at the Morgan Library), and the literature on printed-book

illustration is hardly less extensive. I have nothing to add to accepted knowledge on these topics, and I am not qualified, therefore, to express an opinion on books whose chief claim to beauty rests on "cosmetics" (either in the Greek sense of this word or our own). But there are a few things other than "value criteria" that need to be said about the decoration of the volumes under our consideration. It seems to me just as proper to discuss *what* caused the decoration—*what* warranted or necessitated its use—as it is right for others to analyze and evaluate the nature of it. For example, in direct contradiction to what I have just said about the "sameness" of manuscripts and incunables, we promptly meet up with a sharp differentiation between the two in the matter of the origin of whatever decoration a book may possess. It is manifest that the *original* embellishment of an incunable took place at the instance of the producer (be he the printer, publisher, or financial backer); the decoration of a manuscript, usually (as we have seen) a "bespoke" production,[16] was primarily dependent upon the preferences of the purchaser or owner,[17] not—normally—on the initiative of the vendor, save (perhaps) for the occasional mass-produced volumes. The vendors of incunabula decorated their wares to enhance their value or to make them more attractive (at a higher price) to prospective purchasers; the owners of manuscripts had them decorated in order to illustrate or embellish the contents of their volumes in the particular manner they wished this to be done.[18]

Just now I emphasized the *original* decoration of the book— for it is clear that such beautification could also have been added after the producing firm had completed its work on the copy.[19] This work could either be amateur or professional by nature.[20] Amateur decorating is in need of little comment; it includes the more or less crude marginal figures one often finds in books and manuscripts, and the vigorous though frequently harsh coloring of woodcuts. Professional work can be seen in the more delicate and elaborate coloring of these cuts,[21] so beloved by the Germans, perhaps at the hands of a rubricator, and the sort of "doctoring up" of a volume which one meets with in the case of Antoine Vérard.[22] This Parisian printer,[23] formerly a calligrapher, was particularly partial to treating his vellum copies with an eraser[24] and the paint brush,[25] by means of which he was able to remove the imprint and endeavored to make his woodcuts look like manuscript illumination (which, in a sense, they then were). He seems to have been very successful in palming off these hybrids on British and French royalty.[26] As an energetic bookseller, he did not confine himself to treating only his own publications in this fashion but subjected the productions of other printers (Jean Driard of Paris and Mathieu Latheron of Tours,[27] for example) to similar plastic surgery.

There is, on the other hand, an absolute identity between incunabula and manuscripts so far as the *raison d'être* of their decoration is concerned. It is again self-evident that a figure can be used simply to illustrate the subject under discussion (it could, then, be dispensed with) or it was a vital factor *in* that discussion, in which case it could *not* be treated in so cavalier a fashion. For example, a Vergil or Dante can have illustrations, but the message of the verse is not necessarily rendered any clearer thereby. Indeed, there may be some doubts, philosophically, as to the propriety of such illustrations.[28] How would the author have felt about it? Can any artist, one may well ask, hope to penetrate the special meaning of a cultural document or the nature of a civilization alien or foreign to his own? We have no such faith in the literary critic —and we expect each generation to re-interpret the literary heritage of the past, without ever having any assurance as to what the proper answer may be, or might have been. The fifteenth-century illustrations are quaint, to be sure—but that they help us, or ever helped our forefathers, to understand Vergil any better, I take leave to doubt.[29]

When used as a visual aid,[30] however, the picture represents something controllable, necessary, and comparable. To us (as to mediaeval man, even with his imperfect grasp of the fundamentals) representations of anatomical figures, herbs, animals, views of cities, astronomical configurations, maps, instruments of war, and other familiar or recognizable portrayals implement the written word and are essential to it, whether the volume be a manuscript or a printed text. Botanical treatises and geographical works without explanatory pictures are quite meaningless and incomprehensible. If you should doubt the truth of this assertion, I would refer you to that unillustrated herbal bound in the Morgan "Sammelband" (PML 22222) about which I have discoursed elsewhere.[31]

Then, too, it is possible to use the decoration of books in order that it may tell us something about their history, though evidence of this nature must be used with utmost caution. One of the handiest available means for the printer himself to beautify his volumes was through the use of colored inks, especially (of course) red ink.[32] If an example may be cited, I should like to turn to that controversial book, the *Missale speciale* (inconstantly of Constance),[33] though I hasten to assure the reader that we will not here inquire into the difficult question as to whether it is or is not what I like to believe it is. However, the files of the Kommission für den Gesamtkatalog der Wiegendrucke assure us that in their opinion the book proceeded from the presses of the firm which ultimately became that of Fust and Schoeffer.[34] Now these printers certainly experimented with two different methods of printing in red,[35] both of which proved to be successful;[36] both methods, furthermore, were emulated by other firms working in the fifteenth century.[37] Yet the printer of the Missal, whoever he may have been, used *neither* of these methods—he employed still another process which was demonstrably much more impractical and unsuccessful.[38] It is clear, therefore, that IF the Missal was printed by the parent house, then it was certainly printed no later than 1457—by which time this firm had fully mastered the difficult problem of printing in more than one color.

We may consider, too, the possible pit-falls of using decoration as evidence.[39] A score of years ago, Professor Adolph Goldschmidt[40] discussed the marginal decoration of early Fust and Schoeffer volumes and argued that certain motifs and designs were probably the work of Mainz craftsmen connected with this press. I am certainly not qualified to dispute this demonstration and happily I do not have to contend with the judgment of that grand old man, for it is evident to any one who looks at his plates that Goldschmidt was quite right. But with the bases upon which he founded his judgment I cannot agree. Goldschmidt maintained that, since the foliage of the marginalia included, or rather stemmed from, a log or a branch, this motif had a hidden significance. It was his opinion that this representation was used as a device for concealing the name "Fust," based upon the existence of the Latin word Fustis. But there are two objections to this, so far as I can see. If Johann Fust wished to connect his name with this Latin word, why did he not have the decorators supply a more appropriate representation—say a staff, a club, or a cudgel, which truly represent the meaning of Fustis—rather than a branch or a log, meanings not recorded for this Latin word. If Fust wanted a device, he certainly had an easily recognizable one at hand, since Fust is an unusually current and familiar word based on common West Germanic *Fùsti. Old High German, Middle High and Middle-Low German, and Middle English, all share in the recorded use of Fust. In Modern German, as every one knows, it has become Faust, in English Fist. Did Johann need to look further if he wished for a simple pictorial embodiment of the name Fust which every one would instantly recognize as such?

Professor Goldschmidt argued further that the log or branch, which he believed to be the Fust device, "does not occur in the painted ornament of incunabula after the date of his death in 1466." Now, it has been estimated that there were some 40,000 editions produced prior to 1501,[41] represented by at least a half-million of extant copies. Is it not hazardous to make a sweeping statement embracing all of this enormous and amorphous mass of printed vellum and paper? As a matter of fact, this "device" does occur in the painted ornament of at least one incunabulum after the year 1466. In the very next year (1939) after the appearance of Professor Goldschmidt's article, a bookseller's catalogue listed a copy of Cicero's *Orations* printed at Venice by Adam de Ambergau in 1472.[42] On the first printed page of this copy, there is painted precisely such a log or branch used to support a shield bearing the arms of Hildebrand von Brandenburg, the famous fifteenth-century collector of books,[43] who presented many of them to the Carthusian monastery of Buxheim near Memmingen in Swabia. It may well be true that other books from this famous library include in their decoration a log or a branch cut diagonally to a point at each end, which served as a support for the benefactor's shield,[44] but I have pursued the problem no further than this. Whatever the facts may be, there is certainly no connection of any sort between this Cicero and the decoration which was done for the press of Fust and Schoeffer—and the presence of this particular motif in this particular volume flatly contradicts Professor Gold-schmidt's dictum. But I make no doubt that it is high time to leave off beating the bushes and to return to the bird in our fist: the original decoration of fifteenth-century books.

The printer, as we have seen, made use of colored ink[45] to enhance the appearance of the printed page, and for this purpose he used not only red [46] and blue inks[47] but even, on occasion, gold.[48] In a work now in the Morgan Library, one may observe four differently-colored inks appearing on a single page.[49] Sometimes, however, it seems rather puzzling as to *why* more printing in red was not undertaken. The printer of the 42-line Bible demonstrated his ability to produce headings in red but quickly abandoned this practice.[50] One wonders why he did so, unless it was true that the rubricators, getting wind of what was going on, were causing trouble and insisting that this work was their exclusive prerogative.[51] This might well account for a peculiar feature of the *Consuetudines feudorum* of Obertus de Horto, printed at Strassburg by Heinrich Eggestein on 15 September 1472. Although the heading at the very beginning of the text is printed in red, as also the colo-phon, the other places where rubrics might be expected to ap-pear were left blank by the printer. But Eggestein thoughtfully supplied his publication with a printed leaf of instructions for the rubricator to follow—and some worthy craftsman of the guild has done so most faithfully in the Morgan copy of this edition (PML CL 86).

Color printing was not necessarily, of course, confined to types alone.[52] A printer could also elect to print his cuts in color, printing either the outlines with colored ink[53] or overlaying the normally white surfaces with various colors applied either by a separate run through the press or by means of stencils.[54] Printed border pieces did not always have to be in black, the "white vine" marginalia in the Morgan copy of the 1477 Appianus (GW 2290; PML CL 847) having been printed in red. Sometimes these were impressed by hand after the completion of the printing.[55] Though not always intended to be colored, they were not infrequently painted over with elaborate gold illumination, at least in Italy.[56]

The Germans[57] were especially fond of daubing the woodcuts in their fifteenth-century books with color *after* they had purchased them. The result of this is that the present-day connoisseur, preferring woodcuts "unimproved" in this fashion, is often hard pressed to find such copies amongst the German woodcut incunabula. The coloring in most surviving volumes, clearly the consequence of amateur enthusiasm, is slipshod in the extreme, though professional Briefmaler occasionally performed this service with slightly happier results. Although one also finds French and Italian incunabula touched up with color, this is far less common and only in exceptional cases as crude as in the Northern volumes. Often the coloring in the cisalpine incunables is of truly professional quality.

Besides the use of colored inks, the employment of vellum to preserve the printed message was widely popular;[58] this material was most useful to the printer for the purpose of giving his products a luxurious finish. Printing on vellum[59] is, of course, familiar to all of us, but, up to the present, I have seen no adequate account of what *sort* of books the printers of the fifteenth century saw fit to issue in this fashion. The standard studies on vellum books of *all* periods are the voluminous publications by Joseph Basile Bernard van Praet, whose books are almost as clumsy to use as his name is luxuriant. He divided the books he listed into the five categories: Théologie, Jurisprudence, Sciences et Arts, Belles-Lettres, and Histoire. So far, the division or classification is fine—but after that confusion rapidly becomes confounded. At the end of Tome Cinquième (Histoire), there is a Supplément to all five sections. At the end of this volume, there is a further chapter entitled "Additions et Corrections" to all classes. Tome Sixième comprises a Supplément to the entire work, which is then followed by a chapter on "Acquisitions faites et changemens survenus pendant l'impression du supplément." Nor was van Praet ready to rest there! He concluded his work with a final section of "Additions" to the five groups. In short, there is now a supplement, a supplement to a supplement, a supplement to a supplement to a supplement, a supplement to the fourth degree, and finally a supplement of the fifth power. In view of this somewhat bewildering arrangement, I will not guarantee the precise accuracy of my count in all instances—though for all practical purposes, I think that it is sufficiently correct.

In van Praet's account of the vellum books in the Bibliothèque du Roi[60] (where I have counted only the main body of the catalogue without the supplements), he listed 1,465 *copies*, of which 442 (or thirty per cent of the total) were incunabula, including forty-four duplicates. Now, of the 398 separate editions, no fewer than 198, or almost exactly half of all the

fifteenth-century books, are classed as theology. The next largest
group is that of Belles-Lettres with ninety-one, or nearly
twenty-three per cent. These two categories thus account for
almost three-fourths of the vellum incunables in the library of
the ci-devant Roi. In his other work, treating of vellum books
elsewhere,[61] van Praet listed 1,910 *editions,* of which 396 (or
nearly twenty-one per cent) were incunables. Theology, with
249 entries (sixty-three per cent) easily holds first place, with
Belles-Lettres (seventy-four items or nineteen per cent) again
in second position. In this case, the two pre-eminent groups
claim over four-fifths of the total number. It is evident that, in
the succeeding centuries, theology proved less attractive for
vellum printing than it did in the Quattrocento. In the French
royal library, it will be recalled, incunabula totalled thirty per
cent, but of all the theological works thus printed, the vellum
incunables nearly reached forty-two per cent. For vellum copies
elsewhere, the fifteenth century supplied thirty-five per cent of
all the theological works "sur vélin" listed by van Praet, though
incunabula as a whole amounted to less than twenty-one per
cent of the entire number of vellum editions recorded by this
bibliographer. It is interesting to note, in glancing over van
Praet's report, how much larger (per edition) the number of
vellum copies was in the fifteenth century than subsequently.
Almost sixteen per cent of the "Gutenberg" Bibles are believed
to have been printed on vellum;[62] in the nineteenth and
twentieth centuries, it has not been uncommon to issue less
than a half-dozen copies of an edition in this form.[63]

According to his scheme of classification, the books on vellum
in the "bibliothèques tant publiques que particulières" are
recorded by van Praet in this fashion:

	Total	Incunabula
Théologie	717	249
Jurisprudence	119	28
Sciences et Arts	138	20
Belles-Lettres	734	74
Histoire	202	25
Total	1,910	396

In the case of the vellum books forming part of the former royal library, a summary affords the following result:

	Total	Incunabula	Duplicates
Théologie	475	198	22
Jurisprudence	178	44	5
Sciences et Arts	120	28	3
Belles-Lettres	494	91	9
Histoire	198	37	5
Total	1,465	398	44

The special file of works printed on vellum in the Morgan Library contains a total of 346 entries, divided by centuries in this manner:

Fifteenth century	69
Sixteenth "	81
Seventeenth "	4
Eighteenth "	34
Nineteenth "	106
Twentieth "	52
Total	346

The incunabula and the sixteenth-century books may be classified into these broad categories:

Fifteenth century

Bibles (including separate parts)	8
Classics	6
Devotional and religious works	8
Didactic treatises	2
Humanistic works (3 in Latin)	5
Legal volumes	7
Liturgical books (21 *Horae* and *Officia*)	29
Romances	2
Scientific works	2
Total	69

Sixteenth century

Bibles	2
Classics	3
Devotional books (1 by Luther)	4
Humanistic works (3 in Latin)	13
Legal volumes	8
Liturgical books (38 *Horae* and *Officia*)	48
Scientific works	3
Total	81

Here, the great predominance of liturgical volumes (forty-two per cent in the incunabula and nearly sixty per cent for the sixteenth-century books) may reflect the library's special interest in this field. The vellum books of more recent date include a large proportion of works primarily antiquarian and bibliophilic by nature.

Purveyors of incunabula and manuscripts shared the services of two beauticians of books—the rubricator and the binder. Neither of these need necessarily have been a professional at his job, as we know from the vicar Heinrich Cremer who rubricated and bound the two volumes of the 42-line Bible now in the Bibliothèque Nationale in Paris. His name be blessed for supplying the dates: 15 and 24 August 1456! [64] Another priest (Prester Jacob Carpenter, as we would call him in English) rubricated a Cologne incunabulum before 29 August 1468.[65] Johann Bämler of Augsburg, it seems to me, supplies the necessary evidence for us to conclude that scribes and printers sometimes did their own rubricating.[66] Bämler had worked both as a scribe, since 1453, and as a rubricator, as early as 1466; in Strassburg about the year 1468, he rubricated a number of locally produced volumes. The first precisely dated book from his own Augsburg press was completed on 22 April 1472,[67] but even before this Bämler may have published an *Ordnung zu Reden,* several copies of which he is known to have rubricated.

Professional rubricators also provided the large and handsome initials for the books, the "corpora" as they were called.[68] It is interesting to record [69] that, here too, scribal practice dictated the subsequent usage of the press, for the writers often inserted small letters in the large blank spaces to serve as guides for the rubricators;[70] in the printing industry, these speedily became the traditional guide-letters, serving the same purpose.[71] Initials were not only painted into the manuscripts, they were also stamped in, indeed as early as the thirteenth century.[72] The printer Günther Zainer copied the borders made by the scribe Heinrich Molitor;[73] in turn, woodcut borders[74] frequently served as samples for the work of the rubricator.[75] Again we observe the blurring of that line of demarcation which is supposed to exist between the hand-written and the machine-produced volumes.

Binders and bindings present quite a different problem.[76] When a volume is prized for a binding that is not coeval with its contents, then this object ceases to be worthy of consideration as a book; it becomes a bijou, a bibelot, an objet d'art,[77] or a piece of furniture, depending on its size. Even when the binding of a fifteenth-century book is a contemporary one, its relationship to its contents is often no more than that of a frame to the painting it houses. It may be artistic, it may be beautiful, it may be historic, it may be valuable—but it usually has no genuine connection with the matter which it encloses. In the fifteenth century, manuscripts were often sold unbound in quires,[78] so that they could be decorated and bound to suit the taste of the individual purchaser. Similarly, there seems to have been no "edition-binding," in that period, though some printers did have books bound for their customers when they so wished, at a number of local businesses with which they seem to have had close connections.[79] Nevertheless, books and manuscripts were frequently (perhaps, usually) sold unbound,[80] and they often remained in this condition for years. It is, therefore, only occasionally, and in a limited way, that a binding can be made of service to the historian of books. Incidentally—and just for the record—there is evidence at hand to show that manuscripts were illuminated both before and after binding.[81]

As with the rubricator, we find that scribes and printers could also act as binders[82]—and further to the point, as we have seen, the rubricator himself also bound volumes when he wanted to, Heinrich Cremer having been our example. St. Gall MS. 602 bears an inscription of 1460 which asserts that a certain Cunrat Sailer was the "Schryber und Binder dis Buches." [83] Among the German printers who had once been binders, we may note Konrad Dinckmut, Michael Furter, Konrad Mancz, Johann Schüssler, and George Wirffel. In

Augsburg, Ambrosius Keller bound some fifty-six volumes printed between 1471 and 1476, producing his own first book three years after the last date.[84]

To the professional binder, of course, it made not the slightest difference whether he was binding manuscripts or printed books—if, indeed, he ever paid the slightest heed to what material he had in hand. The binder who worked for William Caxton has left behind him bound manuscripts as well as bound products of the first English press.[85] Often the binder was called upon to bind both manuscripts and printed books together, and he thus created "Sammelbände" of extraordinary interest and rich in promise for the literary or bibliographical historian. Since these volumes are neither "fish nor meat," they fall between two schools of cataloguing.[86] If they are treated as manuscripts, their printed sections are likely to be overlooked —and just the opposite is true when the volume lands on the desk of the printed book department. For years, I have endeavored to call attention to this relatively virgin field for research in a series which I youthfully (and hence formidably) entitled "Libri impressi cum notis manuscriptis." The ninth installment has recently appeared [87]—but if these studies have stirred any profound interest or evoked a following, even faint echoes of this have failed to reach me. Such Sammelbände, particularly those with contents having a common bond of interest, also led to the composite volume which became quite popular with sixteenth-century readers, for example the nearly five hundred folio *De balneis,* which the Giuntas issued from their Venetian press in 1553.

In connection with "books as furniture," I cannot refrain from casting a glance at the library of Jean Grolier de Servin, Vicomte d'Aguisi, whose tastes, if not his library, were formed in the Quattrocento.[88] He was born in 1479, so that by the turn of the century he was a mature man according to the reckoning of his day. His library was extensive, carefully chosen, and beautifully bound[89]—but, so far as my observation has gone, apparently as unread as it was repetitious. At least such volumes from his library as I have seen show few, if any, evidences of much use in Grolier's own life-time. They are indicative of what a gentleman-collector of the time thought was worth binding in the best possible manner, not necessarily what he thought was worth reading. There may be a certain pretentiousness about the books that Grolier had bound so luxuriously. Of the 556 volumes listed in the Grolier Club's edition[90] of the estimable account given by Adrien Jean Victor Le Roux de Lincy (these nineteenth-century bibliographers excelled in long names if nothing else), some 220 or about forty per cent were classical texts, and only seventy-one were in the vernacular. One wonders, too, how seriously the phrase "et amicorum" is to be taken. Grolier could not possibly have let *too* many of his friends borrow volumes from his library or so many of these would hardly be in the immaculate condition that they are today.

Two catalogues provide more general information on what sort of books were considered worthy of sumptuous, or (at any rate) exceptional, bindings. In the recent exhibition of bindings organized by the Walters Art Gallery in Baltimore,[91] eighty-five books of the fifteenth and early sixteenth centuries were shown, of which thirty-nine (or nearly half) were religious, devotional, or liturgical volumes. One solitary scientific book, even by the rather loose standards of those days, appears on the list, accompanied by only four popular books in the vernacular. In his memorable work, Mr. E. Ph. Goldschmidt described fifty-two volumes of this sort, of which more than half (thirty-four in all) were religious works.[92]

The only deduction that I can make from these facts is that then, as now, the work-a-day book—the handy reference work[93] consulted daily or the favorite text to which the reader turns often for pleasure or comfort—was not deemed worthy of elaborate binding. Some few volumes of this sort were, no doubt, read out of existence, but they could not have been numerous, since so few books in such bindings show evidence of heavy use by contemporary readers. De luxe binding was reserved for books intended for display—volumes to be looked at, admired, and destined to remain unopened.[94] Doubtless, many a fifteenth-century reader had a well-thumbed copy of a *Book of Hours* which he, or perhaps his wife, carried to church, but the grandiose display volume reposed at home to impress his friends with the owner's opulence and taste. Sinclair Lewis reminds us that books served the same purpose in twentieth-century America, at least in his mythical Zenith[95] and surely in more real cities, too.

At long last, you may well feel, we have arrived at the chief forms of decoration which the fifteenth-century book enjoyed: illumination and wood- (or metal-) cuts for manuscripts and incunabula. Once again one cannot clearly distinguish between the two, for illumination occurs in printed books and printed illustration in manuscripts.[96] To most bibliophiles, the former statement will be familiar enough, especially in the case of vellum copies,[97] though it may not be so well known that one occasionally finds manuscripts[98] which have been prettied up by having woodcuts pasted into them.[99] This is true, for example, in the Dyson Perrins *Passio Christi* manuscript (Warner no. 123)[100] and a comparable manuscript in the

British Museum (Additional 15712);[101] the Breviary from Kastl of 1454 in the Spencer Collection at the New York Public Library;[102] and Conrad Müller's "Sammelhandschrift" of 1458-1487, now MS. palat. germ. 4 at Heidelberg, which (for a change) has a copper-plate impression pasted in at folio 50.[103] A curious instance is the Scottish *Contemplacioun of Synnaris* by Friar William of Touris, extant in three manuscripts.[104] The volume in the possession of Lord Talbot de Malahide at Dublin (the Asloan manuscript)[105] is in such mutilated condition that it is uncertain what decoration (if any) it once had, but Arundel MS. 285 has seventeen printed cuts inserted into it, one of which is unquestionably from an English printed book of the early sixteenth century (at folio 187). Conversely, the other British Museum manuscript (Harley 6919) is illustrated by a number of unusual drawings in the style of etchings. There are other examples of manuscripts with pasted-in woodcuts, and, though rather infrequently, with woodcuts actually printed into the hand-written volumes.[106] One such manuscript is at Heidelberg (Cod. palat. germ. 438); another was shown in a Munich exhibition of 1938.[107]

Vellum copies of incunabula, it has been said, were often judged worthy to receive manuscript illumination, and both King Matthias Corvinus of Hungary and wealthy Peter Ugelheimer of Frankfurt thought that their copies of the *identical* edition, Torresanus's printing of Aristotle's *Works* (Venice, 1483-84), deserved lavish decoration.[108] Sometimes, too, almost matching illumination is found in several copies of the same work.[109] Thus, the example in the Morgan Library and that formerly belonging to Piero de' Medici (subsequently transferred to the Biblioteca Magliabechiana and therefore now in the Biblioteca Nazionale at Florence) of the *editio princeps* (1494) of the *Anthologia Graeca*, have practically the same marginalia, with extraordinarily similar representations in the roundels.[110] The chief figure is that of Hercules and Antaeus in the center of the lower margin on signature A2 and precisely the same representation is to be found at the same place in the D'Elci copy, now in the Biblioteca Laurenziana at Florence. This is obviously more than just sheer coincidence. Manuscripts, too, display almost identical illuminations in a number of copies as, for example, in several volumes of the French and English texts of Christine de Pisan's *Épître d'Othéa*, of which I have written elsewhere.[111]

The illumination of such incunabula should, one may safely affirm, prove of great value to the art historian, if pursued in a methodical manner.[112] One might suggest an examination of all Florentine incunables obviously decorated in Florence, a cohesive group; such an investigation does not seem to have been attempted in the past on a large scale. The significant thing here, naturally, is the fact that we are thus provided with a group of more or less datable artifacts. In a number of instances, the illumination can be given a very precise "terminus a quo," something valuable in itself for a variety of disciplines.

While illumination was usually the work of a special artist, the scribe himself could sometimes execute drawings, especially simple ones.[113] Thus, Hans Dirmsteyn asserts of himself in a manuscript written in 1471:[114]

> Der hait es geschreben vnd gemacht
> Gemalt, gebunden vnd ganz follenbracht

A number of painters, like the scribes, also took up printing, some with good success like Dominicus de Lapis and Antoine

Vérard; others, such as Johann Zainer and Bartholomaeus Kistler, went bankrupt.[115] The latter, indeed, as with some scriveners, returned to his earlier craft when he realized that printing was not his "dish of tea."

Out and out amateur illustration is sometimes found in both manuscripts and incunabula—as in a written fifteenth-century Neapolitan cookbook, which I happen to own, and in numerous medical texts; as an example of a printed volume with such decoration, one can cite the Morgan copy of the 1473 Schoeffer edition of the *Liber sextus decretalium*.[116] But it is well to recall to mind what an eminent authority on the history of art, William M. Ivins Jr.,[117] said a few years ago, namely that "the typical medieval manuscript was a very sloppy, clumsy, inelegant, unbeautiful thing, hastily and carelessly written and, if illustrated, illustrated with childish drawings." The same thing holds true, one might suggest, for the early printed book, though Robert Proctor solemnly maintained that he had never seen an ugly one among those issued before 1501.

The traditional art of illuminating manuscripts and printed volumes continued to flourish throughout the fifteenth century. Indeed, it seems safe to assert that the artists comprised the group least affected by the invention of printing. After 1450, there was more work for them to do than ever before[118] —more illumination, certainly in the early years; more rubricating; more binding; more pen-and-ink work; more sketching, to be used for woodcuts.[119] Soon, of course, the woodcut book replaced the manuscript with pen-and-ink decoration, as the demand for cheapness grew ever more insistent.[120] Books intended for ecclesiastical purposes, however, continued to be favored for painted decoration. This may be illustrated by an examination of Eric Millar's *English Illuminated Manuscripts of the XIVth and XVth Centuries.*[121] He describes 111 manu-scripts, of which eleven (or ten per cent) are devotional or legal in content and twenty-four (or just under a fourth) are secular texts. The remaining two-thirds of the total are biblical or liturgical volumes. The English humanists[122] were not par-ticularly interested in the physical appearance of their manu-scripts except for John Tiptoft, Earl of Worcester.[123] One wonders if this distaste for, or indifference to, decoration was an indirect result of the iconoclastic beliefs of the Lollards, who exerted such great influence on popular thought in the closing years of the fourteenth century. However that may be, in the second half of the next century, the great English tradition of two hundred years earlier, as exemplified by the work of Mat-thew Paris and William de Brailes, had sunk (in general) to a low level of taste and skill. This may also account for the paucity, and inferior quality, of the illustrations in the early English printed books. In Germany, on the other hand, one notes a remarkable development in the art of woodcut illustra-tion within fifty years, from the crude beginnings at the hands of Albrecht Pfister of Bamberg to the polished craftsmanship of Albrecht Dürer, Ambrosius Holbein, and Hans Burgkmair.[124]

Curiously enough, with regard to illustration, tastes differed sharply as to the sort of manuscripts judged suitable for decora-tion and the type of incunabula thought worthy of artistic embellishment. Legal manuscripts, both Italian and German, often display large miniatures and grandly historiated initials, depicting trials, judges, writers, and other suitable scenes. Though such representations were also painted into legal incunabula,[125] printed illustrations were found to be quite un-necessary or unsuited for these works. The *Gesamtkatalog* records nearly 200 editions of the *Corpus juris civilis*, of which only six have woodcuts—and not one of these comes from Italy.[126] Four of these editions have only a single cut (in one of them, there is also a schematic cut of the "Tree of Consanguinity"); the other two, from Nuremberg, have ten cuts each, of which the later edition is a page-by-page reprint of the earlier. Law books intended for lay readers, such as the several *Reformations*[127] and the *Sachsenspiegel*,[128] were more often decorated in this fashion.

Liturgical books, too, could be lavishly decorated when in manuscript form and then passed over, as unsuitable for illustration, in the case of incunabula. Of Diurnals, 170 editions were issued in the fifteenth century, of which only eight have cuts; a single one, with just two woodcuts, is all that Italy can boast.[129] No fewer than 418 Breviaries were put out by the presses prior to 1501.[130] Many of these, it is true, survive in single copies, imperfect or fragmentary, so that our figures here are not beyond suspicion, even assuming that my count has always been correct. However, only seventy-eight of these editions are listed as being illustrated, of which well over half (forty-nine, to be exact) have only a single woodcut, as often as not portraying no more than some episcopal coat-of-arms. Again, the appearance of such decoration as occurs in the Breviaries is sporadic. The first *Breviarium Herbipolense*, printed at Würzburg by Stephan Dold, George Reyser, and Johann Beckenhub after 20 September 1479, displays a copper-plate coat-of-arms. Thereafter, Reyser was to re-issue the Würzburg Breviary no fewer than five times, but only for the second of these reprintings was use made of the copper-plate, and the other editions are not listed as having any illustrations. Other liturgical books, such as the Missals and the Horae, usually had printed cuts, though here too exceptions can be found. The Constance Missal was produced without even the printed cut of the Crucifixion, usually found facing the beginning of the Canon of the Mass,[131] and an *Officium Beatae Mariae Virginis,* printed at Naples by Mathias Moravus, 10 November 1478, is also devoid of any form of printed illustration.[132] The very fine copy of the *Offices of the Virgin,* produced by the Roman press of In Aedibus Populi Romani in 1571,[133] which was printed on vellum and bound in red velvet (with silver corners, clasps, and coat-of-arms) for the use of Pope Pius V,[134] is also without woodcut illustration, save for a somewhat crude "Tree of Jesse" at the beginning of the text. To compensate for this, the title-page was illuminated with a portrait of the Saint kneeling in prayer before the Virgin and Child.

From a national or local point of view, it may also be enlightening to see what books were thought worth illustrating in a variety of places.[135] Assuming that I have not erred in my count, a rather bold assumption I may say, there are 2,604 editions of German illustrated books listed by Wilhelm Ludwig Schreiber.[136] Books in Latin just manage to nose out German works, the totals being 1,327 to 1,277. The largest single category of such books is that of the schoolbooks with 328, closely followed by scientific literature (except the prognostica) with 318. By a curious coincidence, almanacs, calendars and such like works exactly equal the service books (227 for each). If the prognostica had been treated as scientific texts, as Dr. Arnold C. Klebs chose to regard them, then scientific books would have reached the amazing total of 545 items, well over a fifth of all German illustrated books of the incunabula period.

In the Iberian peninsula,[137] non-Latin incunabula easily

surpassed those printed in that tongue, 550 to 458. As might have been expected from the country of "Los reyes católicos," devotional books to the number of 119 amounted to very nearly a third of the total (374) of Spanish illustrated books. If one added to this figure the thirty-four liturgical books and the twenty-seven Indulgences, then the sum would be 180, nearly half of the total figure. Since Francisco Vindel's recent bibliography of Spanish incunables describes only 984 editions,[138] it surprised me—and may do the same for others—that much more than a third of the entire output of Iberian origin could be classed as illustrated books.[139]

A word of warning, however, is due in regard to figures of this sort! While Ernst Voulliéme listed a total of 1,271 fifteenth-century books printed in Cologne,[140] Albert Schramm included no fewer than 286 illustrated books from there in his vast account.[141] This would suggest that some twenty-two and a half per cent of all the books printed in the Rhenish capital before 1501 were illustrated—but this figure is quite misleading.[142] In order to "brighten up"[143] the numerous textbooks put out by the presses in that city, the printers made free use of "magister cum discipulis" figures. Heinrich Quentell, for example, had six slightly differing cuts of this sort listed by Schramm under his numbers 484 through 489. Figure no. 484 appears in seventy-two editions, and no. 485 in thirty-four printings. In 125 different Cologne books, a single cut of one of these six blocks serves as the sole illustration. Can these books really qualify as woodcut books[144]—when the use of such a cut is as automatic as the appearance of a printer's mark at the end of a volume? Since the printer's mark was also produced from a block, would not all books wherein such a design appears be properly classed as woodcut books, if those with "magister cum discipulis" illustrations are to be admitted to this high honor?

Two samplings from Italy must suffice. Of the 519 Bologna incunables appearing in my checklist,[145] only thirty-six (or seven per cent) were illustrated. Science once again heads the list with fourteen entries. After the turn of the century, more illustrated editions were turned out than formerly in the capital of Emilia. Max Sander listed 276 editions produced there before the middle of the sixteenth century, of which 240 (or about eighty-seven per cent) belong to the Cinquecento.[146]

For Naples,[147] Sander noticed forty-nine illustrated incunabula out of a total of 282 editions produced in that century as recorded by Fava and Bresciano.[148] Thus it is evident that just over seventeen per cent of the Neapolitan incunables were decorated by cuts. The largest single group of illustrated works were, it is instructive to note, books printed in Hebrew. There were fourteen of these against only twelve liturgical volumes and three each for law and science. The survival rate for Hebrew books being as low as it was, one can only suppose that a great many more illustrated editions have utterly disappeared. As the sum total of Neapolitan illustrated books in Sander amounts to 153 items, it is self-evident that over two-thirds of the books included therein belong to the sixteenth century.

While the production of books with printed illustrations was thus on the increase, the hand-illuminated book, whether manuscript or incunable, was rapidly becoming extinct in the closing years of the fifteenth century. In 1491, the Sienese miniaturist Bernardino di Michelangelo Cingnoni bewailed the fact that his art had ceased to be cherished and that books, as they were then made, no longer were illuminated. "Pell' arte mia non si fa più niente—Pell' arte mia è finita per l'amore de' libri, che si fanno in forma che non si miniano più." [149] By the end of the fifteenth century, printing had severely limited the scope of the miniaturists' trade. Proportionately to total book production, fewer volumes were illuminated thereafter in the lavish style employed before 1501. Though this decline in the art of illustrating books by hand may be laid squarely at the door of the press, there is one other conclusion that I beg you to bear in mind. That is, that it was NOT the printing press that finally put the scribe out of business—it was the typewriter.

NOTES
I : The Scribes

[1] Ludwig Hain, *Repertorium bibliographicum* (Stuttgart, 1826-38); Walter A. Copinger, *Supplement to Hain's Repertorium bibliographicum* (London, 1895-1902); Campbell (see note 4 below) under title "Libellus de modo confitendi et poenitendi"; and M.-Louis Polain, *Catalogue des livres imprimés au quinzième siècle des bibliothèques de Belgique* (Bruxelles, 1932). Cited with some frequency in the present study are: Dietrich Reichling, *Appendices ad Hainii-Copingeri Repertorium bibliographicum. Additiones et emendationes* (Munich, 1905-14) and Marie Pellechet [and M.-Louis Polain], *Catalogue général des incunables des bibliothèques publiques de France* (Paris, 1897-1909), abbreviated as Pell. [The Hain, Copinger, and Reichling books will be cited as: H, C, and R].

[2] See also Margaret B. Stillwell, *Incunabula in American*

94

Libraries; A Second Census of Fifteenth-Century Books owned in the United States, Mexico, and Canada (New York, 1940), p. 350, no. M655. [Cited hereafter as *Census*]. The work is cited as *Poeniteas cito* by J. C. T. Oates, *A Catalogue of the Fifteenth-Century Printed Books in the University Library Cambridge* (Cambridge, 1954), p. 643, no. 3883.

[3] The two copies owned in America are listed by Herman R. Mead, *Incunabula in the Huntington Library* (San Marino, California, 1937), no. 5038, and Ada Thurston and Curt F. Bühler, *Check List of Fifteenth Century Printing in the Pierpont Morgan Library* (New York, 1939), no. 1700. [Cited hereafter as: PML CL].

[4] His publications are listed by Marinus F. A. G. Campbell, *Annales de la typographie néerlandaise au XVᵉ siècle* (The Hague, 1874-90) and supplementary editions are given by M. E. Kronenberg, *Campbell's Annales de la typographie néerlandaise au XVᵉ siècle; Contributions to a new Edition* (The Hague, 1956). Studies on Leeu and printing in Antwerp are cited by *Der Buchdruck des 15. Jahrhunderts; eine bibliographische Übersicht herausgegeben von der Wiegendruck-Gesellschaft* (Berlin 1929-36), pp. 62-64.

[5] *La Bibliofilia*, XLII (1940), 65-71.

[6] The manuscript of the *Meditationes* by Johannes de Turrecremata in the University of Pennsylvania Library may be such a work, though this view is not shared by Lamberto Donati, "A Manuscript of 'Meditationes Johannis de Turrecremata' (1469)," *The Library Chronicle*, XXI (1955), 51-60. In modern times, as William H. McCarthy, Jr., has kindly pointed out to me, Moses Polock made manuscript copies for himself of some of the early pamphlets which he sold. His bookshop ultimately became The Rosenbach Company, and these volumes are now in the archives of The Philip H. and A. S. W. Rosenbach Foundation.

[7] Thus the manuscript of Seneca's *Tragedies* in the Bodleian Library (MS. Auct. F. 1. 14—Summary Catalogue No. 2481) is described as "written early in the 15th century in Italy" and also that it "was written for Matthias Corvinus." Corvinus, however, was born at Cluj in 1440 and was King of Hungary in 1458-1490, so that, if the manuscript was written for him, it would seem more likely that it belonged to the second half of the fifteenth century. For the "Summary Catalogue," see note 170 below.

[8] "Das Buch der ersten Jahrzehnte der typographischen Kunst ist in seinen besonderen Erscheinungsformen nicht zu verstehen ohne die Kenntnis der handschriftlichen Buchproduktion des ausgehenden Mittelalters," (Fritz Milkau, *Handbuch der Bibliothekswissenschaft* [Wiesbaden, 1952-59], I, 422). On manuscripts being issued in "editions" of 200 to 400 copies, see Lucien Febvre and Henri-Jean Martin, *L'apparition du livre* (Paris, 1958), pp. 22-23.

[9] Milkau, *op. cit.*, I, 422. Similarly, E. Gordon Duff (*William Caxton* [Chicago, 1905], p. 25) speaks of printing as the "art of writing by mechanical means, 'ars artificialiter scribendi,' as the earliest printers called it."

[10] It is clear that editions set from manuscripts have today the value of prime sources. Those editions that are simply reprints of earlier ones—and differ only in having a few conjectural "emendations"—are of little significance to the literary historian, no matter what value the antiquarian book trade may set upon them.

[11] In a letter to Lucinius Boeticus (Migne, vol. XXII, col. 671), St. Jerome complains of the scribes "qui scribunt non quod inveniunt, sed quod intelligunt; et dum alienos errores emendare nituntur, ostendunt suos."

[12] In his "Prohemye" to the second edition of the *Canterbury Tales* [1484], William Caxton observed: "For I fynde many of the sayd bookes/whyche wryters haue abrydgyd it and many thynges left out / And in somme place haue sette

certayn versys / that he [Chaucer] neuer made ne sette in hys booke" (W. J. B. Crotch, *The Prologues and Epilogues of William Caxton* [Early English Text Society, Original Series 176, 1928], pp. 90-91). A very similar complaint was voiced by Charlemagne as early as 789 (Wilhelm Wattenbach, *Das Schriftwesen im Mittelalter* [Graz, 1958], p. 327). In 1468, at the monastery of St. Florian, two brothers were especially appointed to correct manuscripts against the readings of more correct texts but were enjoined from making emendations based solely upon their own judgments (Wattenbach, p. 337).

[13] In a letter to his brother Quintus, Cicero wrote: "De Latinis uero quo me uertam nescio: ita mendose et scribuntur et ueneunt" (Ep. III. v, Rome: Sweynheym and Pannartz, 1470, f. 33ᵛ—PML CL 598).

[14] *Geographia*, XIII. 1. 54 (Loeb Classical Library, VI, 109-113).

[15] He speaks of the "correctores seu magis corruptores, quia quilibet praesumit mutare quod ignorat" (Karl Christ, "Petia," *Zentralblatt für Bibliothekswesen*, LV (1938), 19).

[16] He describes the contemporary scribe as "doctrinae omnis ignarus: expers ingenii: artis egens" (*De remediis utriusque fortunae*, Cremona: Misintis and Parmensis, 1492—PML CL 1276, sign. f1).

[17] In one of his letters, Aretinus writes: "Mitto tibi Ciceronis orationes in Verrem recte quidem scriptas. Sed ut uidebis male emendatas. Qui enim corrigere uoluit: plane corrupit" (*Epistolae familiares*, II. 12, [Venice: Damianus and Quarengiis], 1495—PML CL 984, sign. b5).

[18] Compare *Troilus and Criseyde*, V, 1793-96 (*The Complete Works of Geoffrey Chaucer*, ed. Fred N. Robinson [Boston and New York, 1933], p. 563).

[19] See *The Donet by Reginald Pecock*, ed. Elsie V. Hitchcock, E.E.T.S., O.S. 156 (1921), p. 7.

[20] Prologue to the *Myrrour of the Worlde,* [Westminster: William Caxton, 1481]—PML CL 1770, sign. a4.

[21] That the spoken word did not necessarily disappear as fast as the scribes and printers chose to believe is illustrated by T. F. T. Plucknett, *Early English Legal Literature* (New York, 1958), p. 114: "What is paradoxical is that these Readings [oral lectures on the law] should have flowered after the introduction of printing into England."

[22] The supply of manuscripts was, apparently, very low in Chaucer's day; cp. Muriel Bowden, *A Commentary on the General Prologue to the Canterbury Tales* (New York, 1948), p. 159. For Wattenbach, see note 12 above.

[23] Roberto Weiss, *Humanism in England during the Fifteenth Century* (Oxford, 1941), p. 115. According to Ludovico Carbone, John Tiptoft, Earl of Worcester, "had spoliated the libraries of Italy" (*ibid.,* p. 117, n. 4).

[24] In the declining years of the fifteenth century, a whole lot of inferior manuscript *Books of Hours* were produced in competition with the occasionally luxurious, printed volumes of this sort. See, also, p. 32. It would be interesting to collect the prices for which these were sold in their own day in order to obtain a relative estimate of the respective value of manuscripts vis-à-vis incunabula. See also note 109, Chapter II.

[25] When Caxton determined to print the English version of Cicero's *De senectute,* he seems to have encountered "grete difficulte" in obtaining a manuscript of this text. Ultimately, a copy, as he tells us, "is with grete instaunce labour & coste comen in to myn honde" ([Westminster]: William Caxton, 1481—PML CL 1772, sign. I2^v-I3). Wattenbach, *op. cit.,* p. 547, speaks of the costliness of manuscripts and that, in 1074, a Missal was judged to be worth a vineyard. That scribes were fond of wine can, in turn, be seen from the colophons which Wattenbach prints on pp. 506 and 516.

[26] General Prologue to the *Canterbury Tales, ed. cit.,* p. 22, ll. 293-296.

[27] See, for example, H. E. Bell, "The Price of Books in Medieval England," *The Library,* 4th ser., vol XVII (1936), 312-332, and Albert Schramm, *Schreib- und Buchwesen, einst und jetzt* (Leipzig, 1922). It is usually assumed that prices (at which manuscripts were sold) "as far as students were concerned, must have been prohibitive" (Francis Wormald and Cyril E. Wright, *The English Library before* 1700 [London, 1958], p. 73).

[28] Wife of Bath's Prologue, *Canterbury Tales, ed. cit.,* p. 98, ll. 634-636.

[29] See my *The Sources of The Court of Sapience* (Leipzig, 1932). Such poets as John Lydgate, Stephen Hawes, Thomas Hoccleve, Christine de Pisan, Matteo Maria Boiardo—and certainly the chroniclers and writers on science—must have been able to consult quite readily a large number of manuscripts.

[30] See Paul Lehmann, "Konstanz und Basel als Büchermärkte während der grossen Kirchenversammlungen," *Erforschung des Mittelalters* (Leipzig, 1941), pp. 258-260.

[31] William Caxton (*Dialogues in French and English* [E.E.T.S., E.S. 79, 1900], p. 38) tells us where the contemporary bookseller got his stocks: "George the booke sellar || Hath moo bookes || Than all they of the toune. || He byeth them all || Suche as they ben, || Be they stolen or enprinted, || Or othirwyse pourchaced." The editor, Henry Bradley, suggests (p. xii) that the French "enprintees" is a mistake for "enpruntes" (borrowed), but this view is not fully endorsed by Henry R. Plomer, *William Caxton* (London, 1925), p. 40.

[32] See Wormald and Wright, *op. cit.,* pp. 26-29. The modern practice of giving art objects and books to public institutions but still maintaining possession of them had a pre-

figuration in the fifteenth century. Thus, in the reign of Henry VI, John Stafford, Bishop of Bath and Wells, presented some ten manuscripts to the church at Wells, which he then proceeded to borrow back for the term of his life; cf. Henry R. Plomer, "References to Books in the Reports of the Historical Manuscripts Commissioners," *Bibliographica*, III (1897), 145.

[33] "By 1362 Petrarch owned perhaps three hundred or more volumes" (Ernest H. Wilkins, "Petrarch's Proposal for a Public Library," *The Boston Public Library Quarterly*, X [1958], 196-202).

[34] See Bell, *op. cit.*, and Wilbur L. Schramm, "The Cost of Books in Chaucer's Time," *Modern Language Notes*, XLVIII (1933), 139-145. After 1480, of course, the manuscript became chiefly a "Luxusartikel" (Hans Wegener, "Die deutschen Volkshandschriften des späten Mittelalters," *Mittelalterliche Handschriften* [Festgabe . . . Hermann Degering, Leipzig, 1926], p. 323).

[35] For further details, consult Mariano Fava and Giovanni Bresciano, "I librai ed i cartai di Napoli nel Rinascimento," *Archivio storico per le province Napoletane*, XLIII (1918), 95-96. The article appeared in the following issues: XLIII (1918), 89-104, 253-270; XLV (1920), 228-250; and LIX (1934), 324-373.

[36] J. C. T. Oates, "The Libraries of Cambridge, 1570-1700" in Wormald and Wright, *op. cit.*, p. 213.

[37] Richard W. Hunt, "Medieval Inventories of Clare College Library," *Transactions of the Cambridge Bibliographical Society*, I (1949-53), 105-125.

[38] Montague Rhodes James, *A Descriptive Catalogue of the Manuscripts in the Library of Peterhouse* (Cambridge, 1899), pp. xxix-xxx and 1-2.

[39] M. R. James, *A Descriptive Catalogue of the Manuscripts in the Library of St. Catharine's College, Cambridge*

(Cambridge, 1925), p. 1. According to James W. Thompson, *The Medieval Library* (Chicago, 1939), p. 387, the inventory of St. Paul's cathedral of 1458 showed a library of 171 volumes, though only fifty-two could be listed in that of 1476.

40 Towards the close of the fifteenth century, the average private library contained fifteen to twenty volumes, mostly manuscripts; cf. Lucien Febvre and Henri-Jean Martin, *L'apparition du livre* (L'évolution de l'humanité, Synthèse collective, XLIX, Paris, 1958), p. 399.

41 Thompson, *op. cit.*, p. 442.

42 Thompson, *op. cit.*, p. 421.

43 In many cases, it is likely "that the collections of manuscripts were regarded as out of date and useless, that they were no longer taken care of and were allowed to disintegrate, and that the remnant was finally thrown away or disposed of to bookbinders" (Hunt, *op. cit.*, p. 109).

44 The same fate befell printed books, of course. The Bodleian Library considered its copy of the First Folio Shakespeare as superfluous when one of the Third Folio of 1664 was received. Together with some other volumes, the book was sold to the Oxford bookseller Richard Davis for £24. Cf. Robert M. Smith, "Why a First Folio Shakespeare remained in England," *Review of English Studies*, XV (1939), 257-264.

45 Johann Georg von Eckhart, *Corpus historicum medii aevi* (Leipzig, 1723), II, 1828: "ipsi boni patres, qui possidebant, aut non intelligebant, aut metuentes eorum praesentia sanctam violari observantiam me rogabant, quatenus omnia illa mihi tollerem, et eis alia quaedam impressa, quae magis optassent, in recompensam redderem."

46 Karl Schottenloher, "Handschriftenforschung und Buchdruck im XV. und XVI. Jahrhundert," *Gutenberg Jahrbuch 1931*, pp. 93-94 and 105.

[47] *Stultifera navis* (Basel: Johann Bergmann, 1 March 1498
—PML CL 1401, sign. b3). In the *Narrenschiff* proper
(Basel: Bergmann, 11 February 1494—PML CL 1397,
sign. a5), one finds the lines:

> Von büchern hab ich grossen hort
> Verstand doch drynn gar wenig wort

[48] "During the Middle Ages books were as a rule the property
of institutions, such as monasteries or cathedral chapters,
and only exceptionally were they to be found in the hands
of individuals" (Roberto Weiss, "The Private Collector and
the Revival of Greek Learning," in Wormald and Wright,
op. cit., p. 112).

[49] Note the *Horae ad usum Sarum* written by John Heath-
field, formerly a huckster [Nomen scriptoris Johannes Heth-
feld quondam caupo] sold at Sotheby's 19 May 1958, lot
77. This is, apparently, the only known manuscript by this
scribe.

[50] This opinion is shared by Wegener, *op. cit.,* pp. 317-318.
A different point of view, namely that the part-time, in-
dependent scribe "made no real contribution to the trade,"
was expressed by John H. Harrington, *The Production and
Distribution of Books in Western Europe to the Year 1500*
(New York, 1956), p. 82. Very probably, few of such
manuscripts got into the trade, though many were certainly written and a certain number of them appeared in
the second-hand market.

[51] Systematically searched were only: Paolo d'Ancona, *La
miniatura fiorentina (secoli XI-XVI)* (Florence, 1914) and
his *La miniature italienne du Xᵉ au XVIᵉ siècle* (Paris and
Brussels, 1925), and the thirty-one volumes of *Serapeum:
Zeitschrift für Bibliothekwissenschaft, Handschriftenkunde
und ältere Litteratur* (Leipzig, 1840-70). Occasional entries
have been made from several of the Vatican and British
Museum catalogues. So far as possible, duplication has
been eliminated in my count.

NOTES

⁵² *A Dictionary of Miniaturists, Illuminators, Calligraphers, and Copyists* (London, 1887-89). The listing extends to the eighteenth century.

⁵³ Some scribes preferred to remain anonymous: "Meum nomen non pono, quia me laudare nolo" (Wattenbach, *op. cit.*, p. 506).

⁵⁴ For example, the *Gradual* for Dominican Use, written by Jacobellus dictus Muriolus of Salerno as his "primum opus" of c. 1270 and the only surviving manuscript signed by this artist; cf. H. P. Kraus Catalogue 88, *Fifty Mediaeval and Renaissance Manuscripts* (New York, [1958]), pp. 66-68, no. 31.

⁵⁵ See the sale catalogue (Sotheby & Co., 9 December 1958), no. 21 (only known MS. by Johannes de Bruolio) and no. 22 (only surviving MS. written by Gaspar Garimberto, 1451).

⁵⁶ "Signed Manuscripts in my Collection: V," *The Book Collector*, I (1952), 79-80: a Palladius *De Agricultura*, written at Verona by Blasio di Girolamo dei Saraceni of Vicenza in 1460. Sir Sydney remarks: "I do not know any other book by this scribe."

⁵⁷ In general, stationers were concerned with *what* the scribes wrote; the scribe was only concerned with *how* he wrote it.

⁵⁸ This is indicated by the shields for the coats-of-arms frequently found empty in Augsburg and Burgundian MSS. The purchaser could have his own arms inserted into the already completed manuscript. On this practice, see Milkau, *op. cit.*, I, 873.

⁵⁹ For an excellent short account on Vespasiano, see E. P. Goldschmidt, "Preserved for Posterity, Some Remarks on Mediaeval Manuscripts," *The New Colophon*, II (1950), 330-332. Interesting details are also given by Vespasiano in his *Vite di uomini illustri del secolo XV* (Florence, 1859).

⁶⁰ Consult Werner Fechter, "Der Kundenkreis des Diebold

Lauber," *Zentralblatt für Bibliothekswesen*, LV (1938), 121-146, with the literature cited there. See also Peter Karstedt, "Eine Erfurter Handschriftenwerkstatt im ausgehenden Mittelalter," *Zentralblatt für Bibliothekswesen*, LIII (1936), 19-29.

[61] Wegener, *op. cit.*, p. 318, who also cites the shop of Gebhard Dacher in Constance. The productions of Conrad Müller of Oettingen are discussed by Hellmut Lehmann-Haupt, *Schwäbische Federzeichnungen* (Berlin & Leipzig, 1929), pp. 98-127.

[62] An account of Shirley is given by Eleanor P. Hammond, *English Verse between Chaucer and Surrey* (Durham, N. C., 1927), pp. 191-194. Raymond Irwin (in Wormald and Wright, *op. cit.*, p. 6) maintains that "there were publishing firms such as that of John Shirley (1366-1456), which produced work in quantity."

[63] The shop of Jean Wauquelin is discussed by Leon M. J. Delaissé, "Les 'Chroniques de Hainaut' et l'atelier de Jean Wauquelin à Mons, dans l'histoire de la miniature flamande," *Bulletin des Musées Royaux des Beaux-Arts* (Brussels, 1955), pp. 21-56.

[64] Cf. Wegener, *op. cit.*, p. 318. For the activity of the dai Libri family in Bologna, see Ludovico Frati, "Gli stazionari bolognesi nel Medio Aevo," *Archivio storico italiano*, 5th ser., XLV (1910), 380-390.

[65] "The Auchinleck Manuscript and a Possible London Bookshop of 1330-1340," *Publications of the Modern Language Association of America*, LVII (1942), 595-627. According to H. S. Bennett ("The Production and Dissemination of Vernacular Manuscripts in the Fifteenth Century," *The Library*, 5th ser., I [1947], 174), "we still lack detailed information about [the professional scriveners'] organization and their day-to-day shop practice."

[66] "From the textual point of view Vespasiano's admirable masterpieces of calligraphy are written with extraordinary

slovenliness. Whole lines are left out, mistakes abound, repetitions are left uncorrected rather than spoil the beautiful page. Vespasiano's manuscripts are written for people who wanted to possess these books, not to read them, and the scribes knew it and were much more attentive to the evenness of their letters than to the sense of what they were writing" (Goldschmidt, *Preserved for Posterity*, p. 331). Strabo (Loeb Library, VI, 112-113) complained of "certain booksellers who used bad copyists and would not collate the texts." It is really surprising to note how few "de luxe" manuscripts show signs of wear.

[67] Wattenbach, *op. cit.*, p. 340. For printers' apologies, see pp. 50-51.

[68] Robinson (1933, p. xxxiii) refers to it as "the best copy."

[69] Wattenbach, *op. cit.*, pp. 475-476.

[70] Wattenbach, *op. cit.*, p. 482. Boccaccio included women in his denunciation of the bad scribes in the epilogue to his *De montibus*, Venice: [Vindelinus de Spira], 13 January 1473—PML CL 734.

[71] Lehmann-Haupt, *Schwäb. Federzeich.*, p. 100. An Italian mystical manuscript, written by a nun in the convent of Santa Croce at Venice in 1500, was offered for sale in Bernard M. Rosenthal's Catalogue IX (Summer, 1959), p. 9, no. 34. Other examples are given by Wattenbach, pp. 444-446. Dyson Perrins MS. 94 was written in 1510 by a nun at the Benedictine Abbey of the Muratae, Florence; cf. catalogue (note 100, Chapter III).

[72] Florence Edler, "The Monastic Scriptorium," *Thought*, VI (1931), p. 201.

[73] Lehmann, *op. cit.*, p. 273. A monk of Melk, Martin von Senging, is known to have written some eight manuscripts in connection with his attendance at the Basel Council (Lehmann, p. 275).

[74] Wattenbach, *op. cit.*, p. 449.

[75] John Gisburgh (1446-49) prefaced his copy of the *Speculum humane vite* (Merton College, Oxford, MS. CCIV) with the remark that it was written "ad utilitatem legencium, videlicet incipiencium, proficiencium, et perfectorum." This clearly identifies the classes of readers for whom the amateur scribe was writing.

[76] "Für die grosse Masse der Studierenden, die Minderbemittelten, ist das Selbstschreiben nach dem Diktat die Hauptquelle der Lehrbücher gewesen" (Christ, *op. cit.*, p. 37).

[77] Oddly enough, only a single book is mentioned in his will; he bequeathed his "breviarium meum magnum" to Giovanni a Bocheta, a priest in Padua (Theodor E. Mommsen, *Petrarch's Testament* [Ithaca, N. Y., 1957], pp. 29-30, 43, and 82).

[78] For example, MSS. Vat. lat. 3195 and 3196; cf. Ernest H. Wilkins, *The Making of the "Canzoniere" and other Petrarchan Studies* (Rome, 1951), pp. 75-79.

[79] Petrarch acquired manuscripts "by purchase, by gift, by having copies made for him or by making copies himself" (Wilkins, *Petrarch's Proposal for a Public Library*, p. 196). On Petrarch's private scribe, see Milkau, *op. cit.*, I, 871, and Hans Widmann, *Geschichte des Buchhandels vom Altertum bis zur Gegenwart* (Wiesbaden, 1952), p. 21.

[80] The state of manuscript writing and of book-buying in general is discussed by Samuel Moore, "General Aspects of Literary Patronage in the Middle Ages," *The Library*, 3rd ser., IV (1913), 369-392.

[81] Cf. Pierre Deschamps, *Essai bibliographique sur Cicéron* (Paris, 1863), p. 74. The MS cost Zomino £ 16/13/6, part of which is itemized thus: "nam pro membranis exposui grossos tredecim, scriptori dedi libras duodecim et cartorario [to the binder] grossos quatuor." Zomino's note is dated: 1 March 1425.

[82] On the copying of manuscripts by Cusanus, see Thompson, *Medieval Library*, p. 463. Consult also Fr. Xav. Kraus, "Die Handschriften-Sammlung des Cardinals Nicolaus von Cusa," *Serapeum*, XXV (1864), 353, 369, and XXVI (1865), 24, 33, 49, 65, 81, 97.

[83] For Chaucer's own copyist, see his poem "Unto Adam, his owne Scriveyn" (*The Complete Works of Geoffrey Chaucer*, ed. F. N. Robinson, p. 628).

[84] Wormald and Wright, *op. cit.*, p. 122.

[85] Weiss, *Humanism in England*, pp. 110, 175, and 123. Gunthorpe also bought printed books; cf. Roger A. B. Mynors, "A Fifteenth-century Scribe: T. Werken," *Transactions of the Cambridge Bibliographical Society*, I (1950), 103.

[86] Hellmut Lehmann-Haupt, "Book Illustration in Augsburg in the Fifteenth Century," *Metropolitan Museum Studies*, IV (1932-33), p. 5.

[87] "Fu Lapo di tenui sustanze, e per questo sono più libri greci e latini ch'egli aveva iscritti di sua mano" (*Vite di uomini illustri del secolo XV*, ed. Angelo Mai [Florence, 1859], p. 509). Of Donato Acciaiuoli, Vespasiano (p. 335) reports: "Aveva la mano velocissima, ed era bellissimo iscrittore di lettera corsiva."

[88] Thus Wilhelm H. Lange, "Buchdruck, Buchverlag, Buchvertrieb," *Buch und Papier* (Festschrift Hans H. Bockwitz) (Leipzig, 1949), p. 61; Widmann, *op. cit.*, p. 26; and Wattenbach, *op. cit.*, pp. 562-563.

[89] "Da nun ausserdem die Gelehrten nicht gerade reiche Leute, die Abschriften aber theuer waren, so haben sie sich ihre Bibliotheken grossentheils selbst geschrieben, wie das namentlich von Boccaccio berichtet wird" (Wattenbach, p. 487).

[90] Fava and Bresciano, *I Librai*, XLIII, 94.

[91] Dorothy K. Coveney, "Johannes Sintram de Herbipoli,"

Speculum, XVI (1941), 336-339, and Theodore C. Petersen, "Johs. Sintram de Herbipoli in two of his MSS," *Speculum*, XX (1945), 73-83. One of the two manuscripts is in the Morgan Library (M 298).

[92] Schottenloher points out that competition arose immediately among the several printers though it did not form part of the scriveners' trade (*Handschriftenforschung*, p. 73).

[93] Carl Wehmer ("Ne Italo cedere videamur," *Augusta 955-1955* [Augsburg, 1955], p. 153) observes "dass schon mit dem ersten gedruckten Buch das Ende der mittelalterlichen Buchkultur gekommen war." The press may have put an end to the mediaeval book—but *not* to the work of the scribes.

[94] Writs continued to be written by hand, and the earliest printed ones seem to belong to the eighteenth century. Late in the sixteenth century, some documents (such as licences) were printed in imitation of the Secretary Hand. Like the printed Indulgences of the fifteenth century, these had spaces left blank to be filled in by hand. See Sir Hilary Jenkinson, "English Current Writings and Early Printing," *Transactions of the Bibliographical Society*, XIII (1915), 273-295.

[95] For scribes at the court in Bologna, see my *The University and the Press in Fifteenth-century Bologna* (Notre Dame, Indiana, 1958), pp. 18-19.

[96] The same situation existed at that time at the University Library Cambridge, where (I understand) new staff-members were expected to learn the hand of the Librarian.

[97] The press certainly put an end to the career of the "Petiarii," though their office had, for some time, been dying out. Since the provisions were by then quite useless, the 1457 Statutes of Perugia suspended the regulations regarding the petiarii: "Nunc vero quia petiarii praedicti non sunt, neque memoria hominum extat tale ministerium hic exerceri, suspendimus praefatum statutum, et rectores a

tali provisione exoneramus" (Guido Padelletti, *Contributo alla storia dello Studio di Perugia nei secoli XIV e XV* [Bologna, 1872], p. 71).

98 See the colophon in Polain, II, 228-229, no. 1576. Jacques de Besançon (George F. Barwick, "The Laws regulating Printing and Publishing in France," *Transactions of the Bibliographical Society*, XIV [1915-17], 70) gave up the illustrating of manuscripts in order to decorate printed books, since it was "needful to make a living."

99 *loc. cit.* This is also the view held by Jan Tschichold, *Schatzkammer der Schreibkunst* (Basel, 1945), p. 5. In 1952, Hans Widmann (*op. cit.*, p. 25) stated: "Der Buchdruck machte ein ganzes Heer von Schreibern überflüssig."

100 Horst Kunze ("Über den Nachdruck im 15. und 16. Jahrhundert," *Gutenberg Jahrbuch 1938*, p. 135) remarks "dass die Handschrift neben dem gedruckten Buche bis weit ins 16. Jahrhundert hinein weiterlebte." Nor did the invention of printing put an end to the trade in manuscripts; see Albrecht Kirchhoff, *Die Handschriftenhändler des Mittelalters* (Leipzig, 1853), p. 41.

101 James Wardrop (article cited in note 107), p. 6.

102 Fava and Bresciano, *I librai*, XLIII, 93.

103 One could sometimes furnish what the other could not. Thus, the manuscript-trade could supply, since the thirteenth century, small portable Bibles, something which the printers did not undertake till the sixteenth century; compare Febvre and Martin, *op. cit.*, pp. 3-4.

104 For the continuation in the trade in manuscripts, see L. M. J. Delaissé, *La miniature flamande* (Brussels, 1959), pp. 76-91, "L'atelier du maître de Wavrin et l'officine de Jean Mielot a Lille."

105 Friedrich A. Schmidt-Künsemüller, *Die Erfindung des Buchdrucks als technisches Phänomen* (Mainz, 1951), p. 100. The production of calligraphic manuscripts ended, of course, the writing of volumes at dictation.

[106] On this point, see S. H. Steinberg, "Medieval Writing-Masters," *The Library*, 4th ser., XXII (1941), 1.

[107] Cf. James Wardrop, "Pierantonio Sallando and Girolamo Pagliarolo, Scribes to Giovanni II Bentivoglio," *Signature*, new ser., II (1946), 7.

[108] Schmidt-Künsemüller (*op. cit.*, p. 95) points out that the humanists retained their own scribes when they were rich enough to permit this luxury.

[109] "The market in medieval manuscripts was in general a bespoke one and the lecturer suggested that perhaps the earliest books manufactured for retail sale in England were the Breviaries and Books of Hours written in Flanders for the English market" (report on Mr. Graham Pollard's Sandars lectures, *Times Literary Supplement*, 20 February 1959, p. 104).

[110] Compare my articles "A South German 'Sammelband' of the Fifteenth Century," *Medievalia et Humanistica*, IV (1946), 107-110, and "A Rhenish 'Sammelband' of the Fifteenth Century," *Traditio*, IV (1946), 429-435. The latter volume contains a text of Italian origin certainly written by a Northern scribe; this may, of course, have been transcribed in Italy (see my "An Anonymous Latin Herbal in the Pierpont Morgan Library," *Osiris*, XI [1954], 259-266). Cf. Mynors, *Werken*, 97.

[111] William Ebesham worked as a scribe both before and after the introduction of printing into England. Thus, some time after 1485, he completed the Westminster Abbey Muniments Book I and its virtual duplicate (College of Arms, Young MS. 72).

[112] Ebesham was a resident of Westminster Abbey when Caxton was printing there; "the connections with his fellow tenant Caxton illustrate the early collaboration, rather than competition, of the professional pen and printing press" (A. I. Doyle, "The Work of a late Fifteenth-Century

English Scribe, William Ebesham," *Bulletin of the John Rylands Library*, XXXIX [1957], 298-325).

[113] Henricus de Colonia, after printing in Bologna, Brescia, Lucca, Modena, Nozzano, Siena, Urbino, and perhaps elsewhere, became a "Briefschreiber" in Rome in 1500 (Konrad Haebler, *Die deutschen Buchdrucker des XV. Jahrhunderts im Auslande* [Munich, 1924], p. 155). For Arnaldus de Bruxella and other printers who resumed their career as scribes, see p. 48 above. Even in the sixteenth century, men worked as scribes and at the press; see, for example, the notes on Bartolomeo Zanetti da Brescia given by F. J. Norton, *Italian Printers 1501-1520; an Annotated List* (London, 1958), pp. XV and 34.

[114] See the Dyson Perrins Sale Catalogue (9 December 1958, pp. 57-58, no. 25). According to Fava and Bresciano, *I librai*, XLIII, 254, "Giovan" wrote many manuscripts but was also an "editore, in società con Mattia Moravo." John Serbopoulos wrote at least three manuscripts of the grammarian Theodor Gaza while residing in England; cf. Weiss, *Humanism in England*, p. 147.

[115] For further notes, consult the references given in the Dyson Perrins Sale Catalogue (pp. 59-61, no. 26). It seems likely that manuscripts could only have been written "on speculation" (as opposed to "bespoke") after the acceptance of the paper codex as a suitable book; compare Rudolf Kautzsch, *Einleitende Erörterungen zu einer Geschichte der deutschen Handschriftenillustration im späteren Mittelalter* (Strassburg, 1894), p. 60.

[116] Wattenbach, *op. cit.*, p. 450. Abbot Kaspar (1426-1461) also had manuscripts written for Tegernsee (Wattenbach, pp. 474-475).

[117] S. H. Steinberg, "Instructions in Writing by Members of the Congregation of Melk," *Speculum*, XVI (1941), 210-215.

[118] Paul Ruf, "Ausgaben des Klosters Benediktbeuern für

Bücher und Schreibzeug von 1495-1510," *Festschrift für Georg Leidinger zum 60 Geburtstag* (Munich, 1930), pp. 219-227.

[119] Ferdinand Eichler, "Eine Salzburger Missalienwerkstätte des späten XV. Jahrhunderts," *Gutenberg Jahrbuch 1940*, pp. 163-168.

[120] Cf. Wehmer, *Ne Italo cedere videamur*, p. 172, abb. 30. It should be pointed out that such manuscripts were still being written a full century after Ratdolt had begun his eminent career as a printer of liturgical books in Augsburg (see Karl Schottenloher, *Die liturgischen Druckwerke Erhard Ratdolts aus Augsburg 1485-1522* [Mainz, 1922]).

[121] For a bibliography of articles on the "Fratres vitae communis," see Milkau, *op. cit.*, I, 872, n. 1; see also Wattenbach, p. 453 ff.

[122] *Gothic and Renaissance Bookbindings* (London, 1928), I, 8, listing the important reference works on the subject.

[123] Alfred W. Pollard, *An Essay on Colophons* (Chicago, 1905), p. 93.

[124] Consult Concetto Marchesi, *Bartolomeo della Fonte* (Catania, 1900), pp. 129 and XXVIII. Marchesi had found sixteen letters by Michelozzi, secretary to Lorenzo de' Medici, "in un codice Magliabechiano e che ho riprodotto integralmente nell'appendice." Naldo de Naldis had been on intimate terms with Lorenzo's secretary and addressed verses to him under the heading: "Ad Nicolaum Michelozium Laurentii Medicis scribam" (cf. Naldus Naldius Florentinus, *Epigrammaton liber*, ed. A. Perosa [Budapest, 1943], p. 2, no. 4).

[125] Compare Weiss, *Humanism*, pp. 86-97, and Mynors, *Werken*, passim.

[126] On Fastolf and Worcester, see the Introduction to my edition of *The Dicts and Sayings of the Philosophers* (E.E.T.S., O.S. 211, 1941), and K. B. McFarlane, "William

Worcester: A Preliminary Survey," *Studies Presented to Sir Hilary Jenkinson* (London, 1957), pp. 196-221.

[127] Cf. my *Dicts*, xlii, n. 2.

[128] Wattenbach, *op. cit.*, p. 545.

[129] See my *University and Press*, pp. 18-19, and Fava and Bresciano, *I librai*, XLIII, 93-94. So did the noble family of Acquaviva (Hermann Julius Hermann, *Miniaturhandschriften aus der Bibliothek des Herzogs Andrea Matteo III Acquaviva* [Vienna, 1898]). A finely written manuscript (c. 1490) of Cicero's *Epistolae ad Brutum et Quintum fratrem*, produced for Andrea Matteo and with his arms in the borders, is now in the Morgan Library (M 403).

[130] James Wardrop, "The Vatican Scriptors," *Signature*, new ser., V (1948), 3-28. See also Raffaello Bertieri, *Calligrafi e scrittori di caratteri in Italia nel secolo XVI* (Milan, 1928). For the French miniaturist (d. 10 Feb. 1557) and his work for Popes Paul III and Julius III, see Nello Vian, "Disavventure e Morte di Vincent Raymond miniatore papale," *La Bibliofilia*, LX (1958), 356-360.

[131] Thompson, *Medieval Library*, 537-542.

[132] As late as 1564, Rüdinger wrote out for him a *Planetenbuch*, having previously (1552) written a *Geomantie* (now Heidelberg, Cod. germ. 833). Consult Carl Wehmer, "Vergessene Bücher aus Ottheinrichs Bibliothek," *Heidelberger Fremdenblatt*, October 1958.

[133] Delaissé, *Miniature flamande*, pp. 182-185.

[134] British Museum Royal MSS. 14 E V and 17 E II. For the printed books, see L. A. Sheppard, "A New Light on Caxton and Colard Mansion," *Signature*, new ser., XV (1952), 28-39, and K. G. Boon, "Was Colard Mansion de Illustrator van Le livre de la ruyne des nobles hommes et femmes," *Amor Librorum* (Amsterdam, 1958), pp. 85-88. See also my review of Sheppard's article (*The Library*, 5th ser., VIII [1953], 53-56), and Alexandre Pinchart, "Miniaturistes,

enlumineurs & calligraphes employés par Philippe le Bon et Charles le Téméraire," *Bulletin des commissions royales d'art et d'archéologie,* IV (1865), 474-510.

[135] Royal MSS. 2 A XVI and 2 B IX (both being Psalters).

[136] Fava and Bresciano, *I librai,* LIX, 327, no. 92.

[137] See Carl Wehmer, "Augsburger Schreiber aus der Frühzeit des Buchdrucks," *Beiträge zur Inkunabelkunde,* neue Folge, I (1935), 78-111, and his additional remarks in *Ne Italo cedere videamur,* passim. Here is also noted (p. 158) a Balthasar Kramer, who wrote a Psalter in 1495 (now Munich MS. Clm 4301).

[138] For general discussions of the problems of printing in Greek and a history of such work, consult Robert Proctor, *The Printing of Greek in the Fifteenth Century* (Oxford, 1900), and Victor Scholderer, *Greek Printing Types 1465-1927* (London, 1927).

[139] Thompson (*op. cit.,* p. 519) points out that most Greek manuscripts of the fifteenth and sixteenth centuries were written by Italian scribes.

[140] Henri Omont, *Georges Hermonyme de Sparte, maître de grec à Paris et copiste de manuscrits* (Paris, 1885).

[141] Weiss, *Humanism,* passim. William Grocyn owned many manuscripts written by Serbopoulos, as well as some transcribed by Emanuel (p. 174). See also Montague Rhodes James, "Greek Manuscripts in England before the Renaissance," *The Library,* 4th ser., VII (1927), 337-353.

[142] Vespasiano da Bisticci, *Vite,* p. 226.

[143] Alexandre Oleroff, "Démétrius Trivolis, copiste et bibliophile," *Scriptorium,* IV (1950), 260-263. Similarly, such a professional scribe as Conrad Müller of Oettingen occasionally wrote a manuscript which was obviously "not for sale." Such a volume is the Sammelhandschrift (now Heidelberg, Univ.-Bibl., pal. germ. 4, written between 1455

and 1479); cf. Lehmann-Haupt, *Schwäbische Federzeich-nungen*, pp. 117-118 and 193-194.

[144] Marie Vogel and Victor Emil Gardthausen, *Die griechischen Schreiber des Mittelalters und der Renaissance* (Leipzig, 1909). For "il Codro" (Antonius Urceus of Forlì), see also my *University and Press in Bologna*, p. 24.

[145] See note 113 above. That trade in Greek manuscripts continued to flourish in the sixteenth century is stressed by Kirchhoff, *op. cit.*, p. 41.

[146] Such as the goliardic verse found in Royal MS. 8 B VI; see description in Sir George F. Warner and Julius P. Gilson, *Catalogue of Western Manuscripts in the old Royal and King's Collections* (London, 1921), I, 221-222.

[147] A characteristic example is given in my article "A Tudor 'Crosse Rowe,'" *Journal of English and Germanic Philology*, LVIII (1959), 248-250.

[148] Much verse of this sort has been printed by Rossell Hope Robbins, *Historical Poems of the XIVth and XVth Centuries* (New York, 1959).

[149] Royal MS. 6 A VIII, written at Spanheim in 1496-97 for Abbot Tritheim.

[150] Royal MS. 10 B XI, a sixteenth-century copy apparently made because no printed text was available.

[151] Sixteenth-century transcripts are found in Royal MSS. 13 B XVII and 13 C II. A copy of similar date of Nennius and the Life of St. Gildas is preserved in Royal MS. 13 B VII.

[152] Fava and Bresciano, *I librai*, XLIII, 94.

[153] Pearl Kibre, *The Library of Pico della Mirandola* (New York, 1936), p. 13.

[154] Fava and Bresciano, *I librai*, XLIII, 94.

[155] *Gesamtkatalog der Wiegendrucke* (Leipzig, 1925-38), no. 872. [Hereafter cited simply as GW].

[156] Royal MS. 13 A VIII is a copy by Petruccio Ubaldino (cf. *DNB*, LVIII, 1) of Florence of the *Scotorum regni descriptio* by Hector Boece, made from the printed edition of Paris, 1526. It was transcribed for Henry Fitz-Alan, Earl of Arundel, and presented as a "strena" on 1 January 1576.

[157] By Johannes Schriber; my number "13.A.8" (*University and Press*, p. 72).

[158] Montague Rhodes James, *A Descriptive Catalogue of the Manuscripts in the Library of St. John's College, Cambridge* (Cambridge, 1913), nos. 48-50.

[159] It is interesting to recall that, even at this late date, Geiler von Keysersberg (1445-1510) preached against manuscripts, especially of the secular sort (Wegener, *op. cit.*, p. 317).

[160] Richard Stauber, *Die Schedelsche Bibliothek* (Freiburg im Breisgau, 1908) and Otto Hartig, *Die Gründung der Münchener Hofbibliothek durch Albrecht V und Johann Jakob Fugger* (Munich, 1917), pp. 261-266.

[161] See my paper "A Fifteenth-century List of Recommended Books," *New Colophon*, III (1950), 48-53. To Dr. Dorothy M. Schullian I owe the excellent suggestion that the author (Marco dal Monte Santa Maria) may not have been thinking of editions at all, and that he here refers simply to texts which he had read and found useful.

[162] For a description of such a manuscript, see p. 87.

[163] "The Miller's Tale," *Works of Chaucer* (ed. Robinson), p. 57.

[164] See my *University and Press in Bologna*, p. 19. The "floating supply" of manuscripts was, probably, quite small, and not nearly big enough for the demand. A market was created through the sale and re-sale of such volumes. Nevertheless, Pier Candido Decembrio thought it necessary to warn Duke Humphrey of Gloucester "that it would be impossible, doubtless for technical reasons, to obtain all the volumes simultaneously" from the list of texts he had

sent to the Duke as important for his library (Weiss, *Humanism*, p. 58). Henry B. Lathrop ("The First English Printers and their Patrons," *The Library*, 4th ser., III [1922], 85) points out that manuscripts were "made to order singly; and the book-trade, with rare exceptions, would be a trade in second-hand books."

[165] Typical of such MSS., one may cite the Aristotle, Cicero, and Seneca in PML 35456 (Bühler, *South German "Sammelband,"* pp. 108-109), the 1495 Venetian Catullus in the National Library at Edinburgh (Hellmut Lehmann-Haupt, "The Heritage of the Manuscript," *A History of the Printed Book . . . The Dolphin III* [New York, 1938], p. 13), and King's MSS. 21 (Cicero), 27 (Horace), 28-29 (Juvenal and Persius), 32 (Martial), and 24 (Vergil) in the British Museum. Twenty dated manuscripts (1461-1491) by the scribe Antonio Sinibaldi are cited by John P. Elder, "Clues for dating Florentine Humanistic Manuscripts," *Studies in Philology*, XLIV (1947), 127-139; see also Stanley Morison, *Byzantine Elements in Humanistic Script* (Chicago, 1952).

[166] Wattenbach, *op. cit.*, p. 448.

[167] *ibid.*, p. 450, n. 5.

[168] "The *Fasciculus temporum* and Morgan Manuscript 801," *Speculum*, XXVII (1952), 182-183, note 29.

[169] James's catalogue, p. 221.

[170] Bodley MS. Arch. Selden B. 10 contains a text of Lydgate's *Proverbes upon the Fall of Prynces* "no doubt copied from the undated edition of 1520(?)." In MS. Rawl. poet. 143, there is included the *Book of Hunting*, attributed to Dame Juliana Berners, which may well be a copy of the Wynkyn de Worde edition of 1496. See the *Summary Catalogue of Western Manuscripts in the Bodleian Library at Oxford* (Oxford, 1895-1953), I, 617, no. 3356, and III, 313, no. 14637.

[171] Compare Montague Rhodes James, *A Descriptive Catalogue*

of the Manuscripts in the Library of St. John's College, Cambridge (Cambridge, 1913), p. 224, no. 187.

[172] A curious example of a somewhat different nature is cited by R. B. Haselden, "A Scribe and Printer in the Fifteenth Century," *The Huntington Library Quarterly,* II (1939), 205-211. Here the scribe has added a manuscript of Gerson's "De statu curatorum et privilegiatorum" at the end of his *Opuscula,* printed at Brussels by the Brothers of the Common Life in 1475. This was copied (perhaps from the Nuremberg edition of about that year—Proctor 2196) "in a contemporary hand and apparently by an extremely skilful scribe, as it exactly and evenly fills the three blank pages [the blank folios 73^v-74^v]. The rubricator was careful to imitate very exactly the style of the initials of the rest of the volume."

[173] James's catalogue, p. 211.

[174] In October, 1488, "he was arrested on a charge of assault committed while leading a gang of some twenty-five young ruffians through the streets of Paris in the previous July" (*Catalogue of Books Printed in the XVth Century now in the British Museum* [London, 1908-49], VIII, xxxviii; work cited hereafter as BMC). Subsequently he became a master of arts, but that he was not wholly reformed seems to be indicated by his publishing, in 1499, "an edition [H 10919] of the notorious 'eroticum' Pamphilus de amore, with an unedifying commentary—the only known production of its kind" (*loc. cit.*). Other printers to languish in jail included Ponticus Virunius at Forlì (Norton, *Italian Printers,* p. 87) and even the great Aldus (cf. Armand Baschet, *Aldo Manuzio. Lettres et documents 1495-1515* (Venice, 1867), pp. III-IV and 27-36.

[175] Compare with the description given by BMC VIII:189.

[176] A few other examples may be cited: MS. It. IX, 188 (6286) of the Biblioteca Marciana, Venice, is a copy of Bartolomeo dalli Sonetti, *Isolario,* [Venice: Anima Mia, n. a.

1485] (cf. *Mostra dei navigatori veneti del quattrocento e del cinquecento. Catalogo* [Venice, 1957], p. 86); Bodley MS. D'Orville 512 seems to be a copy, in part at least, of the Aesop printed at Brescia: Boninus de Boninis, 1487 (Summary Cat. 17390); a Bible in the Rylands Library which may be a copy of the "36-line Bible" is mentioned by Lehmann-Haupt, *Heritage,* p. 8; a manuscript at Yale (Zi + 2073) includes a transcript of Cicero, *Pro Marcello oratio,* [Leipzig: Konrad Kachelofen, n. a. 1492] (I owe this reference to the kindness of Dr. Thomas E. Marston); and the Morgan Library was recently offered a manuscript which included a copy, written on vellum, of Johannes Angelus, *Astrolabium,* Augsburg: Erhard Ratdolt, 1488 (GW 1900; PML CL 379).

[177] "Scriptura enim si membranis imponitur. ad mille annos poterit perdurare: impressura autem cum res papirea sit. quamdiu subsistet? Si in volumine papireo ad ducentos annos perdurare potuerit: magnum est" (*De laude scriptorum,* Mainz: Peter von Friedberg, 1494—PML CL 50, sign. b2).

[178] *loc. cit.* For a good short account of Tritheim, see John F. Fulton, *The Great Medical Bibliographers* [The Rosenbach Lectures for 1950] (Philadelphia, 1951), pp. 2-4.

[179] "Was uns zum Teil bei dieser (CLM 486) und den in den folgenden Jahren (1496 . . .) gefertigten Abschriften Schedels auffällt, ist der Umstand, dass sie aus gedruckten Ausgaben kopiert sind" (Stauber, *op. cit.,* p. 91). Similarly MSS. CLM 212, 386, 435, 648, 962, etc.; consult *Catalogus codicum latinorum bibliothecae regiae Monacensis* (Munich, 1892-94), vol. I. Schedel, of course, bought many printed books as well.

[180] Compare F. Masai, "Le MS 10 de Gand et l'édition incunable, par Thierry Maertens, du discours de Barbaro pour l'élection de Maximilien," *Scriptorium,* III (1949), 80-86.

The printed editions are described by the *Gesamtkatalog* under nos. 3343-46.

[181] Cf. Ferdinand Eichler in *Gutenberg Jahrbuch 1940*, p. 167, and in *Gutenberg Jahrbuch 1941*, p. 68 (cf. note 187 below).

[182] See my "New Manuscripts of The Dicts and Sayings of the Philosophers," *Modern Language Notes*, LXIII (1948), 26-30.

[183] This will also account for the existence of the manuscript copy of the Wycliffite New Testament written out by the antiquary Richard Robinson, about the year 1600, and offered for sale at Sotheby's, 19 May 1958, lot 107.

[184] I am much obliged to Mr. Philip Hofer for permission to cite his manuscript here. The edition was printed by Gabriel Giolito de' Ferrari and there are two copies in the British Museum, viz. 1071.h.4 and G.10390 (*Short-Title Catalogue of Books printed in Italy and of Italian Books printed in other Countries from 1465 to 1600 now in the British Museum* [London, 1958], p. 517). J. G. T. Graesse (*Trésor de livres rares et précieux* [Dresden, 1859-69], I, 189) remarks: "Il existe une contrefaçon de l'édition de 1549 faite à Brescia en 1730 par Faust. Avogadro. La première édition parut à Venise chez Bern. de' Vitali 1533."

[185] See also the curious collection "of beautifully-written manuscript transcripts of rare English books and tracts, Latin and Greek classics, etc." written by John B. Inglis (1780-1870) in twenty volumes, offered for sale by Peter Murray Hill Ltd., Catalogue 67 (Spring, 1959), item 6.

[186] Exemplar. "Exemplar. exempel da man ab schreibt . . . Exemplum. das man ab schreibet" (Wenceslaus Brack, *Vocabularius rerum*, Augsburg: Johann Keller, 1478— PML CL 354, f. liii^v).

[187] Ferdinand Eichler, "Eine Salzburger Prunkabschrift der von Johann Mentelin um 1466 gedruckten ersten deutschen Bibel," *Gutenberg Jahrbuch 1941*, pp. 68-75. For other such

manuscripts (Munich, CGM 204-205 and Wolfenbüttel MS. Aug. fol. I A, I B), see W. Kurrelmeyer, "Manuscript Copies of Printed German Bibles," *American Journal of Philology*, XXII (1901), 70-76.

[188] Fechter, *op. cit.*, pp. 139-140 and 143-144.

[189] For an account of the manuscript, see the description in the modern edition (E.E.T.S., O.S. 168 [1926], pp. xxvi-xxix). Also the copy of this transcript in Queen's College, Oxford, MS. 161 (*ibid.*, pp. xxix-xxx). On the influence of dialect in the writing of texts, see John M. Manley and Edith Rickert, *The Text of the Canterbury Tales* (Chicago, 1940), I, 545 ff.

[190] See my article "The Newberry Library Manuscript of the *Dictes and Sayings of the Philosophers*," *Anglia*, LXXIV (1956), 281-291.

[191] Cf. Curt F. Bühler, "The *Fasciculus Temporum* and Morgan Manuscript 801," *Speculum*, XXVII (1952), 178-183. The same volume contains a manuscript copy of the first edition of the *Cronaca di Partenope* [Naples: Francesco del Tuppo, c. 1486-90]; cf. my study "The Thirteenth Recorded Manuscript of the *Cronaca di Partenope*," *PMLA*, LXVII (1952), 580-584.

[192] Again I am indebted to Dr. Marston for calling my attention to this manuscript (Zi 6937.6). The text is printed on pp. 963-964 of the Basel 1571 edition of the *Opera*.

[193] Cod. bibl. Pal. Vindob. 2706. Compare Ferdinand Eichler, *Gutenberg-Jahrbuch 1941*, p. 68, n. 7, and Friedrich Dörnhöffer, *Hortulus animae* (The Hague, 1907-10), "Elucidations" pp. 10-18. The colophon (III, 1046) reads: "Getruckt vnd geendet zů strassburg durch Martinum Flach ā Mitwoch nach des Heiligen creütz erhöhung Nach d' gebůrt Christi vnsers herrē: M. CCCCC vñ zehen Jar."

[194] This is also entirely different from the life of St. Winifred attributed to Robert of Shrewsbury and printed by Caxton about the year 1485 (PML CL 1787; STC 25853). (STC

= *A Short-Title Catalogue of Books Printed in England, Scotland, & Ireland and of English Books Printed abroad 1475-1640* [London, The Bibliographical Society, 1926]).

[195] See the description in the Summary Cat. No. 21835 and that supplied by Sir Frederic Madden (*Syr Gawayne; a Collection of Ancient Romance-Poems, by Scotish and English Authors* [London, 1839], p. 348: "all, apparently, transcribed from early black-letter editions"). An edition, of which the single sheet in MS Harley 5927 alone survives, was printed by "Thomas Petyt" in London at "Paule Churcheyarde." The manuscript from which John Herbert printed his edition of *Roberte the Deuyll* (London, 1798) was apparently also derived from a lost edition. The Asloan manuscript contains copies of Chepman and Myllar prints which survive today only in imperfect copies in the National Library of Scotland (STC 13166 and 20120); cf. *The Asloan Manuscript, a Miscellany in Prose and Verse Written by John Asloan in the Reign of James the Fifth* (ed. W. A. Craigie; Scottish Text Society, new ser., XIV and XVI [Edinburgh, 1923-25]) and William Beattie, *The Chepman and Myllar Prints; Nine Tracts from the first Scottish Press, Edinburgh 1508* (Edinburgh, 1950), pp. ix-x and xiii-xiv.

[196] BMC IV:5 (IC. 17108). I have consulted the British Museum copy as well as that in the library of Phyllis W. G. Gordan (see her *Fifteenth-century Books in the Library of Howard Lehman Goodhart* [Stamford, Conn., 1955], p. 132); also the example of the 1470 edition in the Museum (BMC IV:10; IC. 17155). The printed volumes were "bene exarata & non mendocissime facta" (1468 ed., f. 2ᵛ); it is further asserted that formerly "non minus ualet pene papyrus uacua & nuda: pergamena ue; quam hodie optatissimi libri emantur . . . ut minoris libri emi fere possint: quam alias soleret redimi ligatura."

[197] MSS. Dd. 7. 1 and 2 of the University Library, Cambridge,

are also copies (Vol. I is dated 9 July 1490) of the Sweyn-heym and Pannartz Jerome (cf. Mynors, *op. cit.*, p. 103), but the manuscript is imperfect at the beginning and it cannot, therefore, be established whether or not the volume ever contained the Letter of the Bishop of Aleria. For a manuscript copy (by the scribe Franciscus Tianus) of the *editio princeps* of Appian's *De bellis civilibus* (Venice: Vindelinus de Spira, 1472—PML CL 731), see Arthur M. Woodward, "A Manuscript of the Latin Version of Appian's *Civil Wars*," *The Library*, 4th ser., XXVI (1945-46), 149-157.

II: The Printers

[1] Actually, one here reads "iouannes" and the date is given as "Die: XII: nouenbris: MCCCCLXXII:".

[2] Compare BMC VI:618 (IB. 27013 and IA. 27017). Joseph van Praet (*Catalogue de livres imprimés sur vélin, qui se trouvent dans les bibliothèques tant publiques que particulières*, [Paris, 1824], II, 215) was badly misled by the colophon, which caused him to comment: Celle [édi-tion] qui est datée de Florence, le 12 novembre 1472, et qui porte le nom de l'écrivain Jean, fils de Pierre de Mayence, n'offre que la date du manuscrit sur lequel elle a été faite. Il en est de même d'une édition italienne des Triomphes de Pétrarque, exécutée d'après un manuscrit du même copiste."

[3] That early printed books were made to resemble manu-scripts is not in the least surprising. In similar vein, it will be recalled that the term "horseless-buggies" aptly described the appearance of the earliest automobiles, which closely approximated the horse-drawn vehicle.

[4] Thus in the four earliest Fust and Schoeffer colophons (BMC I:18-20). Printers were sometimes called "chalco-

graphi" (writers in brass; thus in GW 6064), and printed books have been described as books written with brass (it was Johannes de Spira who "Exscribi docuit clarius ere libros"; GW 6801—PML CL 717). The expression "codices ad stampam" was also used for printed volumes; see Albano Sorbelli, "Enrico di Colonia ed altri tipografi tedeschi a Bologna nel secolo XV," *Gutenberg Jahrbuch 1929,* p. 111.

[5] Compare Roger Doucet, *Les bibliothèques parisiennes au XVIᵉ siècle* (Paris, 1956), pp. 83-89, inventory of 21-28 November 1499, nos. 4-7 vs. 49 & 51. The use of "scripsit" is also noticed by Adolf Schmidt-Künsemüller, *Die Erfindung des Buchdrucks als technisches Phänomen* (Mainz, 1951), p. 100.

[6] See my *University and Press in Bologna,* p. 20. For a most interesting account of Filelfo and his concern with printing, consult L. A. Sheppard, "A Fifteenth-Century Humanist, Francesco Filelfo," *The Library,* 4th ser., XVI (1935), 1-26.

[7] Albano Sorbelli (*I primordi della stampa in Bologna* [Bologna, 1908], p. viii) remarks: "la stampa non è altro, nei suoi inizi, che la continuazione dell' amanuense." That the proper understanding of the prototypographica requires a knowledge of "Handschriftenkunde" is emphasized by Milkau (see note 8 of Chapter I).

[8] As Wattenbach points out in his "Schlusswort" (*op. cit.,* pp. 642-644), the introduction of the press came at just the proper moment, when a material sufficiently cheap (paper) had proved its suitability for the production of books (whether manuscript or otherwise) and a sufficient literate population was at hand. Printing made possible a cheap product to meet a heavy demand. It has even been suggested that printing might have failed of success if paper had not been available (Febvre-Martin, *op. cit.,* pp. 26-27). For Lauber's use of paper in the production of his manuscripts, see Fechter, *op. cit.,* p. 143.

[9] Lehmann (*Konstanz und Basel,* p. 270) suggests that one

124

of the direct results of the Council of Basel was the "Aufblühen" of the paper industry. The industry enjoyed an enormous success so long as the Council lasted.

10 Despite their comment that printing could not have been a success without the availability of a cheap material (paper; see note 8 above), Febvre and Martin assert, on pp. 167-168, that paper was dear and that the cost of it often exceeded the regular printing charges (pp. 171-172).

11 Cf. H. E. Bell, "The Price of Books in Medieval England," *The Library*, 4th ser., XVII (1936-37), 321.

12 *ibid.*, p. 325.

13 Compare Aloys Ruppel, *Johannes Gutenberg; sein Leben und sein Werk* (Berlin, 1947), p. 141. On p. 146, Ruppel suggests that thirty-five vellum copies may have been issued, which required 5,700 skins at a cost of 456 gulden.

14 All surviving copies and fragments of the Psalters and the *Canon Missae*, and practically all of the Durandus and the *Constitutiones*, were printed on vellum (Seymour de Ricci, *Catalogue raisonné des premières impressions de Mayence* (1445-1467) [Mainz, 1911], nos. 54, 55, 61, 65, and 66). Sir Irvine Masson (*The Mainz Psalters and Canon Missae 1457-1459* [London, 1954], p. 6) rightly remarks: "All extant copies and fragments of the 1457 Psalter are folios printed on vellum, as befitted so monumental a venture: the present-day student will scarcely be so aridly minded as to complain at being thereby deprived of the aid, useful in studies of the 42-line Bible, of watermarks." In the case of the *Catholicon*, De Ricci (no. 90) knew of the condition of sixty-one copies, eight of which were printed on vellum.

15 Practically all of the Donatus fragments (if not actually all of them) known to De Ricci were printed on vellum. Of the sixty-one copies of the 1462 Fust and Schoeffer Bible listed by the same bibliographer (no. 79), at least thirty-six vellum ones are recorded.

[16] On the price, use, and availability of vellum, see also Febvre and Martin, *op. cit.*, pp. 4-6.

[17] Vivian H. Galbraith deals mostly with the earlier centuries in his *The Literacy of the Medieval English Kings* (The Raleigh Lecture on History, British Academy, London, 1935). However, he cites (p. 4) an interesting opinion expressed by an Italian visitor to England (c. 1500): "Few, however, excepting the clergy, are addicted to the study of letters, and this is the reason why anyone who has learning, though he may be a layman, is called by them a cleric."

[18] While Jan Tschichold (*op. cit.*, p. 5) implies that writing only became common after the invention of printing, Carl Wehmer ("Die Schreibmeisterblätter des späten Mittelalters," *Miscellanea Giovanni Mercati* [Città del Vaticano, 1946], VI, 152) suggests that laymen could write since the thirteenth century.

[19] Cf. J. W. Adamson, "The Extent of Literacy in England in the Fifteenth and Sixteenth Centuries: Notes and Conjectures," *The Library*, 4th ser., X (1929-30), 163-193: "The conclusion of this paper is that it may be said of the English people of the fifteenth and especially of the sixteenth century that it was by no means an illiterate society and that facilities for rudimentary instruction at least were so distributed as to reach even small towns and villages."

[20] For an excellent account, see the chapter "Correspondence: Private and Official" in Charles L. Kingsford, *English Historical Literature in the Fifteenth Century* (Oxford, 1913), pp. 193-227. As Norman Davis (*Paston Letters* [Oxford, 1958], p. xv) remarks on the prose style of these letters, "it comes so easily to so many people that it must have been common far longer than surviving documents allow us to observe." See also H. S. Bennett, *English Books & Readers, 1475 to 1557* (Cambridge, 1952), *passim*.

[21] At the bottom of his advertisement, William Caxton added the request: "Supplico stet cedula" (William Blades, *The*

Life and Typography of William Caxton [London, 1861-63], II, 101). "The quaint Latin ending, 'Pray don't tear down the advertisement,' was then perhaps a customary formula attached to notices put up in ecclesiastical or legal precincts" (E. Gordon Duff, *William Caxton* [Chicago, 1905], p. 42). It would, of course, have been quite pointless to add this request unless a large body of people could read and understand Latin.

22 Cf. Adamson, *op. cit.*, pp. 164-166. Kingsford (*op. cit.*, p. 195) speaks of the "fantastic spelling and grammar of the *Cely Papers.*"

23 Adamson, pp. 167-168. He maintained (p. 193) that those then able to read were "greatly in excess of the number as frequently, perhaps usually, assumed to-day."

24 Bennett, *English Books*, p. 28, and Wormald and Wright, *English Library*, p. 5.

25 James Gairdner, *The Paston Letters, A. D. 1422-1509* (London, 1904), I, 318. This view is shared by Kingsford, *op. cit.*, pp. 193-196. A contrary opinion was expressed by Emile Legouis and Louis Cazamian, *A History of English Literature* (London, 1926), I, 123, namely that the Paston Letters "cannot be said to show that their writers used the English language easily and fluently. They managed to understand each other, nothing more." Schmidt-Künsemüller (*op. cit.*, p. 91) believes that the amount of literacy has been overestimated: "Nur ein geringer Prozentsatz war des Lesens kundig—wir überschätzen ja zumeist den allgemeinen Bildungsstand dieser Zeit—was aber noch wichtiger ist, die in den ersten Jahrzehnten gedruckten Bücher wandten sich gar nicht an den Bürger, sondern vorwiegend an die Gelehrten und Geistlichen."

26 It is interesting to recall, as Karl Schottenloher does (*Der Buchdrucker als neuer Berufsstand des fünfzehnten und sechzehnten Jahrhunderts* [Mainz, 1935], p. 10), that prior to his invention, Gutenberg had had nothing to do with

books, and that, on the other hand, neither the scribes nor the scriptoria had anything to do with the invention of printing.

[27] Often, of course, they were one and the same. Thus, Pietro Cennini worked as a copyist in the years 1464-74 (José Ruysschaert, "Dix-huit manuscrits copiés par le florentin Pietro Cennini," *La Bibliofilia*, LIX [1957], 108-112), while also correcting texts for his father, the printer Bernardo. For the latter, see BMC VI:xii and Alfredo Servolini, "La stampa a Firenze nel secolo XVº," *Gutenberg Jahrbuch 1956*, pp. 84-90. See also note 113 to Chapter I. That the English scribes made common cause with the printers may be suspected from the fact that the scribal guild, the Stationers, ultimately became the guild of the printers.

[28] Compare BMC VII:xxxviii and George F. Barwick, "The Laws regulating Printing and Publishing in Italy," *Transactions of the Bibliographical Society*, XIV (1919), p. 320.

[29] Cf. Wegener, *op. cit.*, p. 323; Wilhelm Schreiber, "Die Briefmaler und ihre Mitarbeiter," *Gutenberg Jahrbuch 1932*, p. 53; and Arthur M. Hind, *An Introduction to a History of Woodcut* (Boston and New York, 1935), pp. 91, 211, and 279.

[30] Wattenbach, *op. cit.*, p. 644. Though the Brothers of the Common Life at Rostock regarded printing as the "artium omnium ecclesie sancte commodo magistra," nevertheless "in the sixteenth century the doctors of the Sorbonne were much more doubtful on the subject" (Alfred W. Pollard, *An Essay on Colophons* [Chicago, 1905], p. 93).

[31] Albano Sorbelli (*Storia della stampa in Bologna* [Bologna, 1929], p. 6) seems to exaggerate somewhat when he asserts that all the scribes and their colleagues found positions with the press ("tutti trovano un posto nell'arte nuova" and did so "senza proteste di sorta"), but there seems to have been no serious trouble between the scribes and the printers in

that city. As has already been stated (p. 44), there was room for both.

[32] For the careers of Arnaldo da Bruxella (scribe and printer) and Giovan(ni) Marco Cinico (scribe and press-corrector), see Mariano Fava and Giovanni Bresciano, *La stampa a Napoli nel XV secolo* (Leipzig, 1911-12), I, 47-56 and 64-74. See also note 114, Chapter I. Two manuscripts by Cinico are in the Morgan Library (M 389 and M 426; cf. Meta Harrsen and George K. Boyce, *Italian Manuscripts in the Pierpont Morgan Library* [New York, 1953], 50-51, nos. 88-89).

[33] Febvre and Martin (*op. cit.*, p. 174) stress the fact that Hagenau's proximity to Strassburg and Basel probably accounts for its success as a printing center, without taking into account the earlier activity of Lauber's scriptorium in this town. In turn, Kirchhoff (*op. cit.*, p. 117) attributes Hagenau's success as a manuscript center to its nearness to Heidelberg and to the proximity of the Councils of Constance and Basel.

[34] The printer Konrad Mancz and the scribe Andreas Ysingrin were both at work in Blaubeuren in 1477; compare Ernst Voulliéme, *Die deutschen Drucker des fünfzehnten Jahrhunderts* (Berlin, 1922), p. 38, and Wattenbach, *op. cit.*, p. 450.

[35] Voulliéme, *loc. cit.*, p. 96.

[36] Arndes worked as a printer in Lübeck from 1487 until August, 1507, or later; cf. Konrad Burger, *The Printers and Publishers of the XV. Century with Lists of their Works* (London, 1902), p. 14, and Robert Proctor, *An Index to the Early Printed Books in the British Museum* (London, 1898-1903), Part II, Section I, pp. 112-113. From 1498 to 1505, he was employed by the city as a clerk of the court (Voulliéme, p. 96).

[37] Karl Löffler and Joachim Kirchner, *Lexikon des gesamten Buchwesens* (Leipzig, 1934-37), II, 242.

[38] See S. H. Steinberg, "Medieval Writing-Masters," *The Library*, 4th ser., XXII (1941), p. 20, where it is stated, perhaps following Wattenbach (*op. cit.*, p. 489), that a press was in operation in 1501. Proctor (*loc. cit.*, p. 118) merely notes that, in 1522, Wolfgang Stürmer's Erfurt address was "zum bunten Löwen bei Sankt Paul."

[39] Sir Irvine Masson, *op. cit.*, p. 66. See also Kurt Holter, "Ein Reindruck des Canon Missae von 1458 in der National-bibliothek in Wien," *Gutenberg Jahrbuch 1958*, pp. 78-82.

[40] Montague R. James and Claude Jenkins, *A Descriptive Catalogue of the Manuscripts in the Library of Lambeth Palace* (Cambridge, 1930), p. 19.

[41] For example, BMC VIII:84 (IB. 41158) "Imperfect, wanting sheet r3, the text of which is supplied in manuscript rubricated uniformly with the rest of the book"; BMC VIII:140 (IB. 40145) "Imperfect, wanting sheet m2, the place of which is taken by a vellum sheet of manuscript"; BMC VIII:212 (IA. 40884) "Imperfect, wanting sheet D3 (leaves 21,22), the place of which is taken by two leaves of early manuscript supplying text as above"; etc. One of the Morgan copies (PML CL 1820) of John Lathbury, *Liber moralium super Threnis Jeremiae*, [Oxford: Theodoric Rood], 31 July 1482, has the conjugate signatures c1-c8 and x1-x8 supplied in early manuscript, obviously to remedy the printer's lacunae. Similarly the University of Pennsylvania copy (Inc 6763) of the 1474 Padua Hierocles (HC 8545) has leaves A3 and A6 supplied in contemporary manuscript. There are some textual differences between the original print and the MS text; for example, the print (A6^v, line 7) has "dominatōem accipit" where the MS (A6^v, line 2) provides "diminucō3 suscipit," which may be due to hurried reading. I am obliged to Dr. Rudolf Hirsch for bringing this volume to my attention.

[42] Cf. my articles "Variants in English Incunabula," *Bookmen's Holiday* (New York, 1943), pp. 459-474; "Observations on two Caxton Variants," *Studies in Bibliography*, III (1950-51), pp. 97-104; and "The Walters 'Polycronicon' of 1495," *The Journal of the Walters Art Gallery*, XIII-XIV (1950-51), 38-43, 74.

[43] The printer, perhaps by accident, sometimes compensated for lacunae by supplying duplicate sheets or signatures. For example, my copy of HC 8542 (Census H137) lacks sheet m3.6, which is replaced by a duplicate of m1.8. Also my copy of HR 8649 (Census H239) wants signatures c1.2.7.8, which are replaced by the corresponding folios from "e". Here the binder may have misread the signature "e" for the first sheet in this quarto as "c". The University of Pennsylvania copy of GW 2381 (not in Census) lacks first series o1-3, 6-8 but has second series o1-3, 6-8 duplicated, probably the result of faulty storage in the shop.

[44] Thus Richard Garnett's comments on "the influence of the 'traditions of the scribes,' which affected early printing in many ways" and on "the strong influence of the scribe upon the printer" (Introduction to A. W. Pollard's *Colophons*, pp. xvii-xviii). William M. Ivins, Jr. ("Artistic Aspects of Fifteenth-Century Printing," *Papers of the Bibliographical Society of America*, XXVI [1932], 10) similarly remarks: "When people began to print they followed in the trail of the calligraphers. Their letter forms, their page forms, their paper, were all taken over from the makers of handwritten books. So also were their pictures."

[45] *University and Press in Bologna*, pp. 17-18. See also Jean Destrez, *La pecia dans les manuscrits universitaires du XIIIᵉ et du XIVᵉ siècle* (Paris, 1935).

[46] Steinberg, "Medieval Writing-Masters," p. 20.

[47] For the importance of scribal hands to the study of types, see Wehmer, *Ne Italo cedere videamur*. Compare also Ferdinand Eichler, "Monumentalschrift und Frühdruck an

einem Meisterwerk der Schreibkunst erläutert," *Gutenberg Jahrbuch 1937*, pp. 18-23, and Rudolf Juchhoff, "Das Fortleben mittelalterlicher Schreibgewohnheiten in den Druckschriften des XV. Jahrhunderts," *Beiträge zur Inkunabelkunde*, neue Folge, I (1935), 65-77.

[48] Nicola Barone, "Notizia della scrittura umanistica nei manoscritti e nei documenti napoletani del XV° secolo," *Atti della Reale Accademia di Archeologia, Lettere e Belle Arti*, XX, ii (Naples, 1899), p. 6, maintains that the scribes copied Jenson's founts; his types spread throughout Italy "onde i copisti gareggiarono nell'imitarli nella maniera migliore, che essi potevano, sia per far mostra di loro valore calligrafico, sia per tema che l'arte loro non iscemasse a cagione dell'introduzione della stampa." This belief is hotly disputed by James Wardrop, "Pierantonio Sallando and Girolamo Pagliarolo, Scribes to Giovanni II Bentivoglio," *Signature*, new ser., II (1946), 25-26. It is, however, the considered opinion of the distinguished English typographical expert, Stanley Morison, that in the fifteenth century "calligraphy was being affected by typography" (*The Art of Printing* [New York, 1945], p. 35).

[49] See the note on "Printed Specimens of Writing-Masters" in S. H. Steinberg's "A Hand-List of Specimens of Medieval Writing-Masters," *The Library*, 4th ser., XXIII (1943), 194.

[50] Wormald and Wright, *op. cit.*, p. 59.

[51] See my paper "Notes on the Plimpton Manuscript of the *Court of Sapience*," *Modern Language Notes*, LIX (1944), 8-9.

[52] William Blades, *op. cit.*, II, 56-57. See also the present writer's "Lydgate's *Horse, Sheep and Goose* and Huntington MS. HM 144," *Modern Language Notes*, LV (1940), 563-569. The four-page text "De commemoracione defunctorum" is added at the end of the *Flores ex libris de civitate Dei* [Cologne, 1473], to which (of course) it is not textually

related. It will be recalled that Caxton is thought to have learned printing at the press which produced this book (BMC I:234-236).

53 John Lydgate's *Stans puer ad mensam* was printed by Caxton about the year 1479, the edition being a quarto of four leaves (Blades, II, 49-52; copy consulted University Library, Cambridge, Oates 4070). The poem appears on ff. 1-3ʳ, the rest of that page being filled by a group of moral distichs. On ff. 3ᵛ-4ᵛ, there is printed an English metrical *Salve regina;* the remainder of that page contains six proverbial couplets. This seems to be a typical example of the practice of filling otherwise empty pages with a variety of unrelated material, though in this case Caxton may possibly have been following a "Sammelhandschrift." It is surely significant, however, that only two manuscripts have survived which contain the *Salve regina,* in both of which the *Stans puer ad mensam* precedes the other poem, viz. Balliol MS. 354 and Bodley MS. Rawl. C. 48 (cf. Carleton Brown and Rossell Hope Robbins, *The Index of Middle English Verse* [New York, 1943], nos. 2233 and 3074). The Balliol manuscript is certainly a copy of the Caxton edition and the Bodley MS. *may* be another such, though the manuscript has been dated "about 1450" (Axel Erdmann and Eilert Ekwall, *Lydgate's Siege of Thebes,* Part II [E.E.T.S., E.S. 125, 1930], p. 54). Under no. 3074, Brown-Robbins fails to record the Caxton edition.

54 See note 32 of Chapter II. Moravus had himself been a scribe (and a monk); cf. Tammaro de Marinis, "Nota per Mattia Moravo," *Gutenberg Jahrbuch 1930,* pp. 115-118.

55 Fava and Bresciano, *Stampa a Napoli,* I, 74-76.

56 Cf. BMC VI:xiii.

57 Consult Hellmut Lehmann-Haupt, *Peter Schoeffer of Gernsheim and Mainz* (Rochester, N. Y., 1950). The first printer in Ferrara (Andreas Belfortis) also had been a scrivener before he turned to typography (BMC VI:x). A subse-

quent Ferrarese printer, known to us as Severinus Ferrarien-
sis (probably the notary Giacomo Antonio Siverino), was
apparently the same person as the scribe who wrote Trivulziana MS. 86; see Caterina Santoro, *I codici miniati della
Biblioteca Trivulziana*, Milan, 1958, pp. 59-60.

[58] John MacFarlane, *Antoine Vérard* (London, 1900) and
BMC VIII:xxv-xxvii.

[59] Fava and Bresciano, *Stampa a Napoli*, I, 47-56, and BMC
VI:xlii and 857. His printed books are dated between 15
January 1472 and 9 May 1477 (Fava-Bresciano nos. 79 and
98), while MS. lat. 10264 of the Bibliothèque Nationale
contains a number of tracts written by Arnaldus between
22 October 1475 and 26 May 1492 (Léopold Delisle,
"L'imprimeur napolitain Arnaud de Bruxelles," *Bibliothèque
de l'École des Chartes*, LVIII [1897], 741-743). Francesco
del Tuppo was a "scriba regio" at Naples as well as a
corrector and publisher of printed texts (BMC VI:xli and
868). Felice Feliciano worked both as a calligrapher and as
a printer at Pojano (E. P. Goldschmidt, *The Printed Book of
the Renaissance* [Cambridge, 1950], pp. 20-22).

[60] See note 134, Chapter I; Blades, I, 40-41; and Bradley,
Dictionary of Miniaturists, II, 249-250 under "Manchion".

[61] In the Tax Rolls, Schüssler is listed as a "Schreiber" until
1484, although his last printed book is dated 6 March 1473
(Voulliéme, *Die deutschen Drucker*, p. 2).

[62] Cf. Voulliéme, pp. 3-4, and Victor von Klemperer, "Johann
Bämler, der Augsburger Drucker als Rubrikator,"*Gutenberg
Jahrbuch 1927*, pp. 50-52.

[63] As Wehmer points out (*Ne Italo cedere videamur*, p. 150),
the term "Schreiber" must not be taken too literally, since
the Tax Rolls listed under this term all those who were
concerned with the manufacture of books. However, Zainer
seems to have been listed as "Buchtrucker" in and after
1474; doubtless by 1495, a distinction was made between
those who wrote books and those who printed them.

[64] For an estimate of the sort of person attracted by the press at Paris in the fifteenth century, see Febvre and Martin, *op. cit.*, pp. 194-196.

[65] The German Johann of Paderborn (or of Westphalia) worked as a scribe in 1473, the year before he opened his printing plant at Louvain, where he produced some two hundred books prior to 7 November 1496 (the date of his last printed work, Proctor 9240); cf. Alfred W. Pollard, *Catalogue of Books mostly from the Presses of the First Printers . . . collected by Rush C. Hawkins* (Oxford, 1910), p. 280. For further information, see Rudolf Juchhoff, "Johannes de Westfalia als Buchhändler," *Gutenberg Jahrbuch 1954*, pp. 133-136, and Severin Corsten, "Beobachtungen zur Lebensgeschichte Johanns von Westfalen," *Gutenberg Jahrbuch 1958*, pp. 90-95.

[66] William Caxton, too, may have dealt in manuscripts. In the Prologue to his *Blanchardyn and Eglantine* [Westminster: c. 1490], he presents the work to "my lady Margarete duchesse of Somercete," mother of Henry VII: "whiche boke I late receyued in frenshe from her good grace and her commaundement wyth alle For to reduce & translate it in to our maternal & englysh tonge whiche boke I had longe to fore solde to my sayd lady" (*English Incunabula in the John Rylands Library* [Manchester, 1930], plate 5). Since the *Gesamtkatalog* (no. 4402) records only the English version, there may have been no fifteenth-century printing in French. In that event, the volume which Caxton sold to the Duchess of Somerset must have been a manuscript. In Paris, the printer Jean Bonhomme also dealt in manuscripts (Kirchhoff, *op. cit.*, p. 106).

[67] See Charles W. Heckethorn, *The Printers of Basle in the XV. & XVI. Centuries* (London, 1897), pp. 86-112; Voulliéme, *op. cit.*, pp. 33-35; Schottenloher, *Buchdrucker*, pp. 19-22; P. S. Allen, "Erasmus' Relations with his Printers," *Transactions of the Bibliographical Society*, XIII (1916),

297-321; and E. P. Goldschmidt, *The First Cambridge Press in its European Setting* (Cambridge, 1955), pp. 10-11 and 56. On journeymen-printers, see Konrad Haebler, "Druckergesellen in der Frühdruckzeit," *Gutenberg Jahrbuch 1936*, pp. 23-29.

[68] In Leipzig, Melchior Lotter worked as a printer for some forty years, producing an incredible number of books. He died in 1542, being at the time a Ratsherr of his city. [Citations for German printers are taken from Voulliéme and the *Lexikon des gesamten Buchwesens*].

[69] Among other printers who had taken Holy Orders may be cited: Johann Bergmann von Olpe (Basel); Kaspar Elyan (Breslau); Bonetus Locatellus (Venice); Francesco Buonaccorsi (Florence); and Francesco Cenni (Pescia). [Details on Italian printers have been taken from Pollard's Hawkins Catalogue].

[70] BMC VIII:lxxiv and lxxx. At Metz, the Carmelite Johannes Colini practiced "die neue schwarze Kunst" and, of course, at Florence the Ripoli press was operated by the Dominicans.

[71] So was Sixtus Glockengiesser at Lyons (BMC VIII:lii).

[72] In Rome, a press was operated by Joannes Philippus de Lignamine, who may well have been a papal physician and also enjoyed the distinction of being the "first native printer in Italy" (BMC IV:xi). Physician-printers also existed in the sixteenth century; cf. Victor Scholderer, "Heinrich Sybold, Physician and Printer at Strasburg," *Gutenberg Jahrbuch 1954*, pp. 168-170.

[73] The identity of the Ulm printer Hans Hauser (BMC II:544) with the Nürnberg illuminator Hans Hauser and with the woodcutter Hans Husser has been set forth at various times but has not been universally accepted; see Ulrich Thieme and Felix Becker, *Allgemeines Lexikon der bildenden Künstler von der Antike bis zur Gegenwart* (Leipzig, 1907-50), XVI, 141-142, and XVIII, 181, with bibliographies.

NOTES

[74] Thieme-Becker, VI, 282, and Giuseppe Ottino, *Di Bernardo Cennini e dell'arte della stampa in Firenze* (Florence, 1871).

[75] Humanists, too, took up printing, such as Felix (Feliciano) Antiquarius at Pojano, who was a scholar and "an epigraphist of repute, as well as a practitioner of alchemy" (BMC VII:lxxi).

[76] Cf. Domenico Fava, "Le conquiste tecniche di un grande tipografo del quattrocento," *Gutenberg Jahrbuch 1940*, pp. 147-156, and Raffaello Bertieri, *Editori e stampatori italiani del quattrocento* (Milan, 1929), p. 92.

[77] For a good short summary on Cardinal Nicolaus Krebs of Cues, see Ruppel, *Johannes Gutenberg*, p. 81. This phrase is attributed to Cusanus in the preface to the Sweynheym and Pannartz 1468 edition of the *Letters* of St. Jerome (see note 196 to Chapter I). There it is asserted that the Cardinal most earnestly hoped "ut hec sancta ars que oriri tunc uidebatur in germania: romam deduceretur." Febvre and Martin (*op. cit.*, p. 263) state that it was Berthold von Henneberg, Archbishop of Mainz, who described printing as "l'art divin." However, according to Pius B. Gams (*Series episcoporum ecclesiae catholicae* [Leipzig, 1931], p. 290), Berthold von Henneberg only became archbishop on 20 May 1484, so that this phrase could not have originated with him, though he did use it in his censorship proclamation in 1485 (*Archiv für die Geschichte des deutschen Buchhandels*, IX [1884], 238-241).

[78] Compare Karl d'Ester, "Das Werk Gutenbergs und seine Auswirkungen im Urteil der Philosophen," *Gutenberg Jahrbuch 1959*, pp. 45-53.

[79] Not unlike the contemporary views on the radio, television, automation, etc.

[80] Beriah Botfield, *Prefaces to the First Editions of the Greek and Roman Classics* (London, 1861), pp. 146-148.

[81] See my *University and Press in Bologna*, pp. 15-16.

82 "Veneti enim impressores adeo inculcaverant ac foedaverant hoc divinum opus ut non modo Cornelianae facundiae majestas inquinaretur, sed vix sensus ullus conjectari posset" (Botfield, p. 162).

83 In a letter to Johannes Andreae of 17 May 1470 (*Epistolarum familiarium libri XXXVII* [Venice, 1502], fol. 221), Filelfo urged the Cardinal to continue his useful efforts: "Pergite igitur, ut coepistis, noliteque prius a tam liberali: fructuosissimoque, labore conquiescere, quam latinos omnis codices: lectione dignos, quam emendatissimos reddideritis." For the other letters of Filelfo, see Sheppard, *Filelfo,* p. 10 and p. 14; also note 91 below.

84 Petrus de Ancharano, *Repetitio c. Canonum statuta de constitutionibus,* 3 August 1493 (GW 1628; Bühler 36.A.4), fol. 34.

85 "Si quid tamen in eo mendae et erroris insertum fuerit: non impressoris negligentia: sed potius famulorum incuria pretermissum putes" (Nicolaus Burtius, *Bononia illustrata,* 1494 [GW 5794; Bühler 19.A.48; PML CL 1211, fol. 38]).

86 See the Prologue, facsimiled and translated (by Antje Lemke), in *Aldus Manutius and his Thesaurus Cornucopiae of 1496* (Syracuse University Press, 1958). Aldus also asked his readers to assume that he was not responsible for possible faults ("mendosorum enim est exemplarium culpa, non mea").

87 Seymour de Ricci, *A Census of Caxtons* ([London], 1909), plate for type 4*, from the Epilogue of his edition of *Charles the Grete,* 1 December 1485. Similar remarks will be found in the Prologues to the *Golden Legend* and the *Book of the Knyght of the Toure.* An amusing colophon is translated by Pollard (*Colophons,* 109-110) from a volume printed by Corallus at Parma (HC 14984): "Should you find any blots in this work, excellent reader, lay scorn aside; for Stephanus Corallus of Lyons, provoked by the ill will of certain envious folk who tried to print the same book,

finished it more quickly than asparagus is cooked, corrected it with the utmost zeal, and published it, for students of literature to read." See, also, Victor Scholderer, "Citius quam asparagi coquuntur," *Gutenberg Jahrbuch 1931*, pp. 107-108.

88 "Petrus cenninus Bernardi eiusdem Filius quanta potuit cura & diligentia emendauit ut cernis. Florentinis ingeniis nil ardui est." (Colophon at the end of the *Bucolica;* HCR 14707; PML CL 1097). Cf. note 74 above.

89 The printers, of course, were frequently no more learned than the scribes; compare Petrarch's opinion cited in note 16, Chap. I. Type could be set by compositors who did not properly understand the language in which they were working; see my "At thy Golg first eut of the Hous vlysse the saynge thus," *Studies in the Renaissance,* VI (1959), 223-235.

90 As Garnett has observed, the printer was often "very decided in asserting his superiority to the copyist, a reaction, perhaps, against a feeling entertained in some quarters that the new art was base and mechanical in comparison with the transcriber's, with which, in the estimation of the devotee of calligraphy, it could only compare as a motor-car may compare with an Arab steed" (Pollard, *Colophons,* p. xix). See, for example, the lines in the unsigned Lucan ([Venice: Printer of Basilius, 1471]—Census L260) printed in *Gutenberg Jahrbuch 1937,* p. 72, n. 3.

91 For a full account, together with an English rendering of the text, see Sheppard, *Filelfo,* 24-26. Some years later (1524), according to Herbert of Cherbury, Cardinal Wolsey argued that one "could not be ignorant what diverse effects this New Invention of Printing had produced. For as it had brought in and restored Books and Learning, so together it hath been the Occasion of those Sects and Schisms which daily appeared in the World, but chiefly in *Germany;* where men begun now to call in question the present Faith and

Tenents of the Church, and to examine how far Religion is departed from its Primitive Institution." We are also informed that Cardinal Wolsey "sent to have the rarer sort [of books] copied out of the Popes Library." Cf. Edward Lord Herbert of Cherbury, *The Life and Reign of King Henry the Eighth* (London, 1683), p. 147; PML Acc. no. 6396. Donald G. Wing, *Short-Title Catalogue of Books printed in England . . . 1641-1700* (New York, 1945-51), II, 177, does not seem to record this imprint, which reads: "Printed by *M. Clark,* for *H. Herringman,* and are to be sold by *T. Passenger* at the three Bibles on *London Bridg,* MDCLXXXIII."

[92] Pollard (Hawkins Catalogue, p. xxvii) points out that "many of the men who took up the new art were probably well advanced in life. The printer had not only to live on his resources while making his lengthy preparations, but to meet all sorts of expenses, and finally to pay a heavy bill for paper. To do this required capital, and the possession of capital is more often the attribute of age than of youth." A different point of view is taken by Febvre and Martin (*op. cit.,* pp. 111, 164-165, and 172), who assert that little capital was needed except for the necessary investment in type ("chaque série de poinçons, chaque fonte même, représente une petite fortune"). Particulars on financing, especially in regard to the Strozzi family of Florence, are given by Florence Edler de Roover, "New Facets on the Financing and Marketing of Early Printed Books," *Bulletin of the Business Historical Society,* XXVII (1953), 222-230.

[93] Compare Rudolf Blum, *Der Prozess Fust gegen Gutenberg* (Wiesbaden, 1954). It is assumed that Fust lent Gutenberg two sums of 800 gulden each, which with interest (plus interest on the unpaid interest) amounted to 2,020 gulden by November 1455. See also my reviews of Blum's book in *Renaissance News,* VII (1954), 37-40, and in *Papers of the*

Bibliographical Society of America, XLVIII (1954), 283-288.

[94] Ruppel, *Gutenberg,* p. 165.

[95] Wehmer, *Ne Italo cedere videamur,* p. 151.

[96] Compare Paul Schwenke, *Johannes Gutenbergs zweiund-vierzigzeilige Bibel; Ergänzungsband zur Faksimile-Ausgabe* (Leipzig, 1923), and Ruppel, *Gutenberg,* p. 143.

[97] He was born on 9 January 1449 and died 30 April 1512; cf. Anton Steichele's edition of Wittwer's "Catalogus Abbatum monasterii SS. Udalrici et Afrae Augustensis," *Archiv für die Geschichte des Bisthums Augsburg,* III (1860), 11-12.

[98] Details from Robert Proctor, "Ulrich von Ellenbog and the Press of S. Ulrich at Augsburg," *Bibliographical Essays* (London, 1905), p. 84. According to Febvre and Martin (*op. cit.,* pp. 163-164), presses were cheap but the instances they cite belong to the sixteenth century.

[99] Augustinus de Ancona, *Summa de potestate ecclesiastica* (H 960; Census A1213).

[100] Voulliéme, *Die deutschen Drucker,* p. 3.

[101] "Paper was the major item in book production costs" (De Roover, *op. cit.,* p. 227).

[102] Compare p. 42 and note 13 to Chapter II, and figuring the vellum required by each copy as costing just over eleven gulden.

[103] *op. cit.,* p. 47. The cost of vellum for thirty-five copies is there set at 450 gulden.

[104] Since it is assumed that Gutenberg actually received only 1,600 gulden and that the rest of the money demanded by Fust represented interest on the loan, then 420 gulden was only the increment and not money available to the printer for use in the business.

[105] "Du XVI ᵉ au XVIII ᵉ siècle, chaque 'presse' comporte une équipe de quatre ou cinq ouvriers: d'ordinaire un ou deux

compositeurs, deux pressiers, et un apprenti qui fait les commissions et exécute les menus travaux" (Febvre and Martin, p. 197).

[106] Ruppel (*op. cit.*, p. 143) envisages a *minimum* force of eighteen employees.

[107] In addition to the Bible, Gutenberg is assumed at least to have begun the printing of the 1457 Psalter. If this be so, it is probable that some of the presses—in any event, one press—with a full complement of operators operated for a period longer than two years. Exactly how long the Gutenberg presses were active is, of course, anybody's guess.

[108] Wehmer, *Ne Italo cedere videamur*, p. 151.

[109] Compare Ruppel, p. 172, and Wehmer, *ibid.*, p. 156. Hieronymus Holzschuher (1469-1529), Nuremberg patrician, bought his copy of the *Vocabularius juris utriusque*, Basel: [Michael Wenssler], 20 Aug. 1483, for one gulden in 1490 (E. P. Goldschmidt Catalogue no. 114, item 295). The *Gesamtkatalog* (GW 5400) records the same price for a copy of the Venice, 10 Feb. 1495/96, edition of the *Breviarium Moguntinum,* bought at the Frankfurt autumn fair in 1498 by Job Rohrbach. For the contemporary prices of a variety of manuscripts, printed books, and certain commodities, see Schmidt-Künsemüller, *op. cit.*, pp. 98-103.

[110] Johannes Reuchlin's salary was only one hundred gulden as a member of the Privy Council to the Elector Palatine Philip towards the close of the century; see the article on him in the *Quarterly Review,* CLXXXVIII (1898), 1-30.

[111] Pollard (Hawkins Catalogue, pp. xxiii-xxiv) reminds us that rent may have been no small item in the printer's budget. In hiring a house, he was obliged to select "a strongly built one, as the old presses were kept steady by being placed between supports which reached from floor to ceiling, so that thick beams would be needed if the clumsy screw was to work quietly."

[112] For his views on Gutenberg's means and probable expenses, see the reference given in note 96 above.

[113] As Pollard significantly observes (Hawkins Catalogue, pp. xxvii-xxviii), it is "remarkable that of upwards of 350 printers who began work before the close of 1480, not more than ten per cent. continued in business for as much as twenty years, and several of these are lost to sight for considerable periods and then reappear, as if they had been driven by want of capital to work for other men, and subsequently started again on their own account. If we take another test of success, quantity of production, we find that only about the same proportion of printers are known to have completed 100 books."

[114] Konrad Haebler (*Typenrepertorium der Wiegendrucke* [Halle, 1905-24]) lists 159 separate firms. Eight anonymous firms have been singled out from the group of "unsigned" books; these are not included in the above total.

[115] "Anton Koberger, de Nuremberg, peut-être le plus puissant éditeur de son temps, et qui fit paraître, de 1473 à 1513, au moins 236 ouvrages, d'ordinaire très importants et d'une typographie impeccable, pratiquait la même méthode [that is, specialization in the shop as practiced by Aldus]" (Febvre and Martin, *op. cit.*, p. 186). Konrad Burger (*Printers*, pp. 137-140) lists 248 books which Koberger issued before 1 January 1501.

[116] See note 95, Chapter II.

[117] Blades, I, 75, and Crotch, pp. cxxvii-cxxix, supply the Caxton details.

[118] "In der Tat konzentrierte sich das Buchgewerbe anfangs in den wichtigsten Handelszentren Deutschlands, Italiens und Frankreichs, nicht in den Universitäten, Klöstern oder fürstlichen Residenzen. Die neue Kunst war von Beginn an eine Angelegenheit des Bürgertums, die Träger der mittelalterlichen Kultur, Kirche und Adel, waren an ihr nicht beteiligt" (Schmidt-Künsemüller, *op. cit.*, p. 91). A

similar view is expressed by Schottenloher (*Buchdrucker*, p. 14), and a contrary one by Febvre-Martin (p. 272): "La présence d'une Université, ou d'une juridiction souveraine, en France d'un Parlement, avec tout ce que cela représente de clientèle sûre: tel est donc bien souvent ce qui attire, au XVe et au XVIe siècle, les imprimeurs et les libraires, telle est l'origine de beaucoup de centres typographiques importants."

[119] It has been estimated that some 40,000 editions were printed, approximately three-fourths of which were books. Printed book production prior to 1501 probably amounted to some six million copies, of which slightly more than half a million have survived to our day; cf. Carl Wehmer, "Zur Beurteilung des Methodenstreits in der Inkunabelkunde," *Gutenberg Jahrbuch 1933*, pp. 267 and 281-282, and Kurt Ohly, "Der gegenwärtige Stand der internationalen Inkunabelinventarisierung," *Beiträge zur Inkunabelkunde*, neue Folge, I (1935), 29. Ernst Consentius holds that this figure is much too low and that probably another 10,000 editions were produced which have totally disappeared ("Die Typen und der Gesamtkatalog der Wiegendrucke; eine Kritik," *Gutenberg Jahrbuch 1932*, pp. 82-87). A lower estimate is given by Febvre and Martin (*op. cit.*, p. 377): "30 à 35.000 impressions différentes exécutées entre 1450 et 1500 sont parvenues jusqu'à nous."

[120] By 1472, the market was glutted with books and many printers were forced into bankruptcy (cf. my *University and Press in Bologna*, p. 28, n. 63). Febvre-Martin (p. 114) state that this situation was again prevailing a score of years later (unless 1492 is merely a misprint for 1472).

[121] Wehmer, *Ne Italo cedere videamur*, p. 152. Blades (I, 74) estimated that Sweynheym and Pannartz had produced 12,000 volumes in five years, and William Caxton's output has been thought to be in excess of 10,000 (Rudolf Hittmair, *William Caxton, Englands erster Drucker und Verleger*

[Innsbruck, 1931], p. 46). In his day, the population of London was probably about 50,000 (C. Creighton, "The Population of Old London," *Blackwood's Magazine,* CXLIX [1891], 477-496). Carl Wehmer (*Gutenberg Jahrbuch 1933,* p. 281) gives these population figures: Lübeck and Cologne, 20,000 to 30,000; Nürnberg, Strassburg, and Ulm, c. 20,000; Augsburg, 18,000; and Basel, 7,000. For further estimates, see Schmidt-Künsemüller, *op. cit.,* p. 97. It is hardly surprising that an overproduction of books quickly followed the introduction of the press.

[122] Even some copies of the early Fust and Schoeffer Psalters remained unsold for ten or twelve years (Masson, *op. cit.,* p. 5). There is some evidence that books remained "in print" for relatively long periods; see, for example, note 42 above in regard to the English *Polycronicon.* The *Astrolabii canones* ([Venice: Paganinus de Paganinis, c. 1497]—GW 2759) was still available for purchase in 1512, when a dated supplementary note was printed on the title-page. The *Rosa anglica practica medicinae* by Johannes de Gadesden, Pavia: [Girardengus and] Birreta, 24 Jan. 1492 was re-issued with some leaves reprinted on 12 May 1517 (Proctor-Isaac 13910). See also the comment under Census P329.

[123] Abbot Tritheim spoke of the volumes "qui impressoria jam arte in omnem diffusa terram multipliciter dietim profunduntur in lucem," Eckhart, *op. cit.,* II, 1829.

[124] Oskar von Hase, *Die Koberger* [Leipzig, 1885], p. LXXXIV.

[125] At first, naturally, the printers did not have their own guilds. Those in Basel mostly joined the "Safranzunft" (Voulliéme, *Die deutschen Drucker,* pp. 18-35), while at Strassburg, on 26 November 1502, it was decided that the printers should belong to the guild "zur Stelze," to which painters and goldsmiths had previously belonged (Schottenloher, *Buchdrucker als neuer Berufsstand,* p. 31).

[126] Similarly, the firm of Sweynheym and Pannartz in Rome was dissolved in 1474, and in the same year Vindelinus de

Spira temporarily gave up his Venetian press. Though two years later Vindelinus reopened his press, this seems to have met with little success, for the new venture did not last more than a few months.

[127] See Voulliéme (p. 81 and elsewhere); also Fritz Juntke, "Marcus Brandis und die Agenda Merseburgensis," *Gutenberg Jahrbuch 1944-49*, pp. 97-99.

[128] Carl Wehmer, "Augsburger Schreiber aus der Frühzeit des Buchdrucks, II: Heinrich Molitor," *Beiträge zur Inkunabelkunde,* neue Folge, II (1938), 114. Molitor belonged to the "habenitzen" and paid no tax save the "stuira minor" (head tax); cf. Wehmer, *Ne Italo cedere videamur,* p. 151.

[129] On the printers' financial problems, see Febvre and Martin, *op. cit.,* p. 173 ff. Wilhelm H. Lange ("Buchdruck, Buchverlag, Buchvertrieb," *Buch und Papier* [Festschrift Hans H. Bockwitz; Leipzig, 1949], p. 74) points out that the printer had to face terrific competition, whereas the scribe had practically none. He also describes the various financial ills which could beset the printer.

[130] It is also noteworthy that "we find Jacobinus Suigus printing one book at Sangermano in 1484, one book at Vercelli in 1485, one book at Chivasso in 1486, and these three books constitute the total output of incunabula at the places named" (Pollard, Hawkins Catalogue, p. xxx).

[131] Cf. my *University and Press in Bologna,* p. 42.

[132] For an excellent account, see Anatole Claudin, *Origines de l'imprimerie à Albi en Languedoc (1480-1484); les pérégrinations de J. Neumeister, compagnon de Gutenberg, en Allemagne, en Italie et en France (1463-1484)* . . . (Paris, 1880).

[133] "The Strasbourg *Speculum iudiciale,* 1473: with a Note on the Career of Johann Bekenhub," *The Library,* 5th ser., XI (1956), 273-277. Voulliéme favors the spelling: Beckenhub.

[134] The frequent absence of colophons in the earlier incunables is identical with the scribes' wish for anonymity; see note 53 to Chapter I.

[135] *op. cit.,* pp. 43-45, 48. Consult BMC VII:lxxviii on the peculiar problem as to whether Bazalerius de Bazaleriis actually printed books in Reggio Emilia, as he claimed to have done.

[136] Consider the curious instance of the *Breviarium Vratislaviense* (GW 5512), whose colophon informs us that the book was printed in Venice, 17 August 1499. Actually the Breviary was printed at Nuremberg by Georg Stuchs and the GW adds the note: "Als Vorlage diente wahrscheinlich eine verlorene Venetianer Ausgabe, deren Druckort (und Druckdatum?) irrtümlich übernommen wurde." Stuchs, of course, was an old hand at printing and produced some twenty-one Breviaries before 1501, of which this is his penultimate edition. Is it likely that he would have made such a primitive mistake? Is it not equally possible that Stuchs wanted to take advantage of the printing reputation which Venice held in this field and simply tried to pass off his copies as products of the Republic in order to promote their sale? Can this explanation also apply to the Besançon Missal (W. H. James Weale and Hanns Bohatta, *Catalogus Missalium ritus latini ab anno M.CCCC.LXXIV impressorum* [London, 1928], p. 31, no. 176) which, the colophon states, was printed in Venice by Jacques Maillet, 14 April 1500? The Missal was, of course, produced by this printer in Lyons; cf. BMC VIII:lix. Filelfo's *Consolatio ad J. A. Marcellum* has the note "Impressum Romae kalendis Ianuarii. M.cccc.lxxv," because the author wished it to appear as a Roman publication. Actually it was printed in Milan by Philippus de Lavagnia; cf. BMC VI:703 and Sheppard, *Filelfo,* 7-10.

[137] Consult Dennis E. Rhodes, "More Light on Fifteenth-century Piracies in Northern Italy," *Gutenberg Jahrbuch 1958,* pp. 96-98.

[138] A typical example is the edition of Eusebius, *De evangelica praeparatione*, Venice: 10 November 1500. According to BMC V:435, "the attribution [to Bartholomaeus de Zanis] of this book, which Proctor (no. 5102) assigned to Locatellus, is uncertain." However, a colophon found in some copies asserts that the volume was printed by De Zanis for Octavianus Scotus and that it had already been printed off on 3 November 1498, when the edition was temporarily suppressed. GW 9445 adds the note: "Anscheinend traten beim Verkauf Schwierigkeiten ein, vielleicht infolge des im Jahre vorher dem Bernardinus Benalius gewährten Privilegs (vgl. Nr 9444). Wohl deshalb wurde der Druck zwei Jahre später mit einem neuen Kolophon versehen." De Zanis worked at Venice, publishing books between 31 January 1486/7 and 3 February 1513. "In the sixteenth century he issued a steady stream of books" (F. J. Norton, *Italian Printers, 1501-1520* [London, 1958], p. 162). Also there was issued at Portese on 20 August 1490 an edition of its *Statutes*, on which De Zanis had been engaged since 15 October 1489, this being "the only early book printed at Portese" (BMC VII:1115). Yet on 31 March 1490, there appeared an Italian *Legenda aurea* (Reichling 1659) with the note "stampate in Venetia per Bertolamio de Zani de Portesio," indicating that De Zanis' press continued in operation. Again one wonders if De Zanis might not have printed the book in Venice for sale in his native Portese, since it seems an unusually impractical method to build a new press to publish a single work of eighty-four leaves. According to GW VII: col. 654, Petrus Apianus of Ingolstadt re-issued in 1536 the remainder of a Donatus first printed by Mathis Hupfuff not before 1505. See also note 136 above.

[139] A most singular error in dating occurs in the edition of the *De origine et gestis Francorum compendium* put out by Pierre Le Dru. "The date 'nonagesimonono' in the subscription to the author's verses on 135ᵃ has been struck

through with a pen and 'nonagesimo quinto' written above it, the ink much faded. Similar corrections are found in other copies and the error is also noticed in the errata" (BMC VIII:190).

[140] "The Fifteenth-century Editions of Petrarch's *Historia Griseldis* in Steinhöwel's German Translation," *The Library Quarterly,* XV (1945), 231-236. Another such edition was probably one of the two Zainer editions of the *Pestbuch* (Arnold C. Klebs, *Incunabula scientifica et medica* [Bruges, 1938], nos. 933.1 and 933.3). Liturgical works printed in one diocese in the "use" of another represent books definitely intended for export.

[141] Thus the *Biblia latina, cum glossa ordinaria Walafridi Strabonis,* issued shortly after 23 September 1481; cf. GW 4282.

[142] For example, the *Biblia cum postillis Hugonis de Sancto Charo* of [1498-1502]—GW 4285.

[143] Proctor-Isaac 14286 and 14293 will serve as examples.

[144] Konrad Burger, *Buchhändleranzeigen des 15. Jahrhunderts* (Leipzig, 1907), nos.: 2-5, 7-9, 11-14, 16-20, 22, 24, 26, 30-31, and Ernst Voulliéme, "Nachträge zu den Buchhändleranzeigen des 15. Jahrhunderts," *Wiegendrucke und Handschriften* (Festgabe Konrad Haebler; Leipzig, 1919), pp. 18-44, nos. 1-4.

[145] "I think we may take it for granted that we really have little or no conception of what the contents of a book-dealer's shelves were like in some such year as 1495" (William M. Ivins, Jr., "Artistic Aspects of Fifteenth-century Printing," *Papers of the Bibliographical Society of America,* XXVI [1932], 3).

[146] Four in Latin and nine in German.

[147] Two in Latin and four in German.

[148] For example, that in British Museum MS. Addit. 28752, f. 1, reproduced by Burger, *Buchhändleranzeigen,* no. 1. Another listing of Lauber stock, in the dialect of Augsburg,

is bound in Heidelberg MS. pal. germ. 314, according to Wegener, *op. cit.*, p. 318. See especially Fechter, *op. cit.* (note 60, Chapter I).

[149] Although Febvre and Martin (*op. cit.*, p. 174) discuss Hagenau as a printing center, they fail to point out that Lauber had a "manuscript-factory" there long before the introduction of the press.

[150] "Hie hat der tutsche psalter ein ende des frowent sich myn diebolt loubers hende" (Wilhelm Eule, "Kaufmännische und betriebswirtschaftliche Entfaltung des Buchgewerbes im 15. Jahrhundert," *Archiv für Buchgewerbe und Gebrauchsgraphik,* LXXII (1935), 342).

[151] For instructive figures on book production at various places, see Febvre and Martin, *op. cit.*, pp. 278-281. The account of Hebrew printing (pp. 405-409) is particularly valuable.

[152] Of the remaining five, three come from Strassburg, and two from Nuremberg; cf. GW 4295-4306.

[153] See the summary printed by GW IV: col. 679.

[154] For a revealing summary of what was—and what was not—printed in Bologna, see my *University and Press in Bologna,* passim.

[155] Febvre and Martin (*op. cit.*, p. 107) point out that the public soon came to prefer printed books to manuscripts. Schmidt-Künsemüller (*op. cit.*, p. 102) states that, until 1480, manuscripts and incunables cost about the same, so that whatever preference there may have been, this was not based on economic factors.

[156] *Vite di uomini illustri,* p. 99. Andrea Matteo III Acquaviva (1458-1529) lived in the era of the incunabula. Nevertheless, he had at least fourteen manuscripts, mostly in Greek, written out for him. He also established a press in his Neapolitan palace, under the supervision of Antonius de Frizis. Here he printed the Plutarch, *De virtute morali* (1526), from a manuscript in his possession. A vellum copy, with gold printing and illuminations perhaps the work of

Rinaldus Piramus of Monopoli, is in the Morgan library (Acc. no. 25128). See also Hermann J. Hermann, *Miniaturhandschriften aus der Bibliothek des Herzogs Andrea Matteo III Acquaviva* (Vienna, 1898).

[157] For the opposite point of view, see Max Sander, *Le livre à figures italien depuis 1467 jusqu'à 1530* (New York, 1941), IV, xix. He suggests that the aristocracy of Italy "grands bibliophiles, n'avaient aucune compréhension du nouveau procédé de la production mécanique des livres. Ils considéraient le livre produit en masse comme quelque chose de plébéien, indigne d'un grand seigneur, comme de la camelote, bonne tout au plus pour la populace. Cela ne pouvait pas être admis dans leurs bibliothèques où il n'y avait place que pour le manuscrit, l'objet unique, le personnel, le précieux."

[158] Compare Josef Fitz, "König Mathias Corvinus und der Buchdruck," *Gutenberg Jahrbuch 1939*, pp. 128-137.

[159] University Library, Budapest, Cod. lat. 4. Incidentally, this manuscript does not contain the Corvinus coat-of-arms but that of Beatrice of Aragon, thus proving that even this noble family was willing to own such codices; cf. Fitz, *loc. cit.*

[160] Vienna, National Bibliothek, Cod. lat. 564 and Budapest, Magyar Nemzeti Muzeum, Cod. lat. 347 (Fitz, *loc. cit.*).

[161] The *Missale Strigoniense*, Nürnberg: Anton Koberger, 31 August 1484 (HC 11429; copy at PML, Acc. No. 46497), was issued under the patronage of Corvinus. Fitz calls this "die Erstausgabe," though Weale-Bohatta tentatively list three earlier editions not seen by them (nos. 1487-89). The Breviary is described under GW 5468; for other books issued under royal patronage, see Fitz's article.

[162] Giovanni Pico della Mirandola, *Opera omnia* (Basel, 1572-73), II, 403-404: "Nunc Martianum Capellam & Senacae [*sic*] quaestiones naturales opto, si modo emaculati sint codices, nam qui apud nos sunt opera Sybillae indigent,

eos si impressos emere possim gratius mihi erit, sin minus non longo postliminio tui ad te redibunt."

163 Dorothy M. Robathan, "Libraries of the Italian Renaissance," in James W. Thompson, *The Medieval Library* (Chicago, 1939), p. 581. On Beroaldus's concern for the press, see my *University and Press in Bologna*, pp. 38-39.

164 Pearl Kibre, *The Library of Pico della Mirandola* (New York, 1936), p. 3.

165 Cf. p. 41 and note 83 above. Filelfo wrote (*Epistolae familiares* [Venice, 24 Sept. 1502], f. 229): "Fieri certior abs te cupio, pater modestissime, & qui libri istic imprimantur: & quae singulis sint pretia constituta. Nam satis eos esse emendatos, labore, diligentiaque tua, ex codicibus nonnullis, aduerti. Itaque rogo te: ut me propediem, hac de re, commonefacias."

166 Cardinal Domenico della Rovere (1440-1501) had incunabula as well as manuscripts decorated "dai migliori artisti del minio del suo tempo" (Domenico Fava, "Libri membranacei stampati in Italia nel Quattrocento," *Gutenberg Jahrbuch 1937*, p. 64). See Fava's article for examples of other Italian noble families.

167 When he was obliged to raise money in 1481, Ferdinand pawned his library of 266 books to Baptista Pandolfini, a Florentine "mercatore" at Naples. Of this total, at least fifty books (over eighteen per cent.) were incunabula, according to the annotation "in stampa" appended to the entries. The original document is in the Bibliothèque Nationale, ms. nouv. acq. lat. 1986; cf. Henri Omont, "Inventaire de la bibliothèque de Ferdinand I er, roi de Naples (1481)," *Bibliothèque de l'École des chartes*, LXX (1909), 456-470.

168 Maria Bertòla, "Incunabuli esistenti nella Biblioteca Vaticana durante il secolo XV," *Miscellanea Giovanni Mercati*, VI, 398-408 (Studi e testi 126; Città del Vaticano, 1946). The famous copy of Gratian's *Decretum* (HC 7886) of the

Museo di Schifanoia, Ferrara, belonged to Bishop Lorenzo Roverella († 1474) of that city; cf. *Mostra storica nazionale della miniatura: Catalogo* (Florence, 1954), no. 608.

[169] In twenty-three years, Abbot Tritheim purchased for the abbey of Spanheim "non sine magno labore et multis impensis . . . circiter duo millia volumina tam scripta, quam impressa" (Eckhart, *Corpus historicum medii aevi*, II, 1828).

[170] Also in France. For Vérard's sale of books to Henry VII of England, see p. 70 and note 25, Chapter III; those to French royalty are briefly noted in footnotes 22 and 23 of the same chapter.

[171] The pertinent literature on the German humanists is cited by Thompson, *Medieval Library*, p. 470.

[172] "At the beginning of the 16th century the Benedictine monastery of Tegernsee alone possessed several thousand incunabula, besides more than 2,000 MSS." (Ernst Weil in a book-review, *The Book Collector*, VII [1958], 431).

[173] Cf. Edmund Bishop, *Liturgica historica* (Oxford, 1918), pp. 431-433; Thompson, *op. cit.*, p. 435.

[174] "In Rome he also made large purchases of printed books, particularly from the press of Sweynheim and Pannartz" (Weiss, *Humanism in England*, p. 152); see also Percy S. Allen, "Bishop Shirwood of Durham and his Library," *English Historical Review*, XXV (1910), 445-456. Two Italian humanists active in England, Stefano Surigone and Pietro Carmeliano, apparently enjoyed close relationships with the printers Theodoric Rood and William Caxton (Weiss, *Humanism*, p. 172).

[175] Included in the inventory of John Paston's books (James Gairdner, *The Paston Letters* [London, 1904], VI, 65-67) is item 4 "a Boke in preente off the Pleye off the [Chess]." This must surely refer to one of the two Caxton editions of Jacobus de Cessolis, *The Game and Playe of the Chesse* (E. Gordon Duff, *Fifteenth Century English Books* [Lon-

don, 1917], nos. 81 and 82), and some of the other entries may also refer to printed texts. The Pastons, of course, hired William Ebesham to write manuscripts for them, and his bill is printed by Gairdner (V, 1-4). The passage omitted by the editor is supplied by Norman Davis, *Paston Letters* (Oxford, 1958), pp. 67-68.

[176] Dennis E. Rhodes, "Don Fernando Colón and his London Book Purchases, June 1522," *Papers of the Bibliographical Society of America*, LII (1958), 231-248.

[177] The papal collector Giovanni Gigli purchased in London in 1477 his copy of the Diodorus Siculus, *Bibliothecae historicae libri sex*, Venice: Andreas de Paltasichis, 31 January 1476/77 (GW 8375); confer Thomas E. Marston, "A Book owned by Giovanni Gigli," *The Yale University Library Gazette*, XXXIV (1959), 48. Gigli may also have purchased in England the copy of the 1472 Venetian edition of Cicero's *Tusculanae quaestiones* (GW 6890), which found its way into the library of Bishop John Moore (1646-1714) and thence into the Cambridge University Library as the gift of King George I in 1715 (cf. J. C. T. Oates, *A Catalogue of the Fifteenth-Century Printed Books in the University Library Cambridge* [Cambridge, 1954], p. 291, no. 1633).

[178] But his son Guidobaldo possessed at least one incunable printed on vellum; see Domenico Fava, *Gutenberg Jahrbuch 1937*, p. 64. See also E. P. Goldschmidt, *The Printed Book of the Renaissance* (Cambridge, 1950), p. 3n.

[179] See Max Husung, "Aus der Zeit des Übergangs von der Handschrift zum Druck; 1. Matteo Battiferri als Miniaturist und als Bibliophile," *Mittelalterliche Handschriften* (Degering Festchrift; Leipzig, 1926), pp. 155-157, with colored plate of the *Anthologia Graeca*. The Albertus Magnus edition is described under GW 716 and Klebs 24.1.

[180] For notes on the Morgan vellum copy, see pp. 85-86 above, and note 110, Chapter III.

181 He had worked for the Ripoli press, first as a "garzone," then as a "compositore allo stampare," and finally (15 May 1483) contracted, as a "socio," for the printing of the *editio princeps* of the Latin Plato (HC 13062—PML CL 1166); cf. Emilia Nesi, *Il diario della stamperia di Ripoli* (Florence, 1903), pp. 16-17, 27-28, and 57-58.

III: The Decorators

1 See my article cited in note 168, Chapter I.

2 For a discussion of the various Ratdolt editions, see my "The Laying of a Ghost? Observations on the 1483 Ratdolt Edition of the *Fasciculus temporum*," *Studies in Bibliography*, IV (1951-52), 155-159. By 1480, the work was available in England, for Caxton [or some one else?] used the text for the continuations of the *Chronicles* of England for 1419-1461. What edition was consulted has not, so far as I am aware, been investigated. Perhaps such an edition as Louvain: Jan Veldener, 29 December "1476" [i. e., 1475— cf. Census R248], for Caxton is known to have had contacts with Veldener (Duff, *Caxton*, p. 27). However, Kingsford (*Eng. Hist. Lit.*, p. 119) suggests that the text "was adopted by Caxton" and that it "has passed commonly under his name," which at least leads one to assume that Kingsford believed Caxton to have been merely an editor, not the compiler of the continuation. This view is shared by GW (VI: cols. 477-478).

3 Just as manuscripts were copied from incunabula, so cuts were used as models for painted or drawn illustrations. Consult, for example, Hellmut Lehmann-Haupt, "Die Holzschnitte der Breydenbachschen Pilgerfahrt als Vorbilder gezeichneter Handschriftenillustration," *Gutenberg Jahrbuch 1929*, pp. 152-163, which deals with two manuscripts

(Gotha, Chart. A. 541 and Karlsruhe, cod. St. Peter, Papier, 32) illustrated with drawings based on those made by Erhard Reuwich for Breydenbach's *Peregrinatio in terram sanctam* (GW 5075). The illustrations in the Heidelberg Bidpai manuscript of c. 1485 (pal. germ. 466) are dependent on the cuts in the [Urach: Fyner, 1481-82] (BMC II:612 and H 4028) and the Ulm: Holle, 1483 (H 4029) editions of the *Directorium humanae vitae;* cf. Lehmann-Haupt, *Schwäb. Federzeich.*, p. 171. The Fyner editions belong to his Urach press, not to the Esslingen one as reported by Lehmann-Haupt; see my "Notes on Conrad Fyner's Press in Urach," *Gutenberg Jahrbuch 1936*, pp. 63-72. One wonders if those in MS. Royal 14 D 1 were copied from the Abbeville 1486 *Cité de Dieu* (GW 2891), since the miniatures in the manuscript are said to "represent" the same subjects; compare the Warner and Gilson catalogue, II, 138. The Spencer Collection of the New York Public Library owns a manuscript copy of the printed edition (Ulm: Johann Zainer, [a. 15 August 1473]) of the German *De claris mulieribus* by Boccaccio. Here the original woodcuts have been carefully copied, though unimportant minor variations have been introduced.

[4] See Elizabeth Mongan and Edwin Wolf, 2nd, *The First Printers and their Books* (Philadelphia, 1940), p. 13, where the work is assigned to Haarlem, perhaps because the cuts were made by a Haarlem woodcutter. The book is usually given to Utrecht; cf. Henry Bradshaw, *Collected Papers* (Cambridge, 1889), p. 269 and *Treasures from the Pierpont Morgan Library* (New York, 1957), p. 26, no. 46.

[5] See p. 46, and notes 41 and 42 of Chapter II for examples.

[6] For the extent and use of xylography, see Febvre and Martin, *op. cit.*, pp. 53-59.

[7] GW 8674-9034. The woodcut editions are described by Konrad Haebler, "Xylographische Donate," *Gutenberg Jahrbuch 1928*, pp. 15-31. See also Friedrich-Adolf Schmidt-

Künsemüller, "Ein unbekannter xylographischer Donat," *Gutenberg Jahrbuch 1958,* pp. 78-83.

[8] *Einblattdrucke des XV. Jahrhunderts* (Halle, 1914), p. 7.

[9] De Ricci, *Census of Caxtons,* p. 68, no. 55.

[10] Johannes Mauburnus, *Rosetum exercitiorum spiritualium et sacrarum meditationum* [Zwolle: Pieter van Os], 1494 (CA 1224; Oates 3617; PML CL 1655), has on the title-page a xylographic heading, verses printed from movable type and a woodcut illustration from a block previously used to print the blockbook *Cantica canticorum;* cf. William M. Conway, *The Woodcutters of the Netherlands in the Fifteenth Century* (Cambridge, 1884), pp. 11, 201, and 337.

[11] For example, such Vérard editions as the Merlin *Prophecies* [1503, though dated "1498"], the *Tristan chevalier de la table ronde* [c. 1506], and the *Gestes romaines* [c. 1508] described under nos. 549, 555, and 556 of the *Catalogue of Manuscripts and Early Printed Books . . . now forming Portion of the Library of J. Pierpont Morgan* (London, 1907).

[12] Since Vavassore worked from 1515 to 1572, his undated works are hard to place. His *Opera nova intitolata dificto di ricette* has the date 1541 (Davis and Orioli, catalogue 161 [1959], item 210). Consult also Leo Bagrow, *Giovanni Andreas di Vavassore, a Venetian Cartographer* (Jenkintown, 1939); The John Carter Brown Library, *Report to the Corporation of Brown University, July 1, 1958* (Providence, 1958), pp. 47-55; and my brief mention in *Papers of the Bibliographical Society of America,* LII (1958), 150.

[13] Just as the scribes had done, some painters took up printing (e.g., Erhard Reuwich; cf. Voulliéme, *op. cit.,* pp. 112-113 and Thieme-Becker, XXVIII, 80 [Reeuwich]). Another such person was Bartholomaeus Kistler of Strassburg; subsequently he sold his equipment to Mathis Hupfuff and went back to painting (Voulliéme, p. 158; Thieme-Becker,

XX, 390). The printer Johannes Bämler of Augsburg has been identified with the painter and miniaturist of that name active in Augsburg from 1453 to 1504 (Thieme-Becker, II, 340). See the two miniatures executed by Johannes "Bemler" in 1457 in the Morgan Library (M 45; Meta Harrsen, *Central European Manuscripts in the Pierpont Morgan Library* [New York, 1958], pp. 68-69). The miniaturist is listed under the name Hans Balmer in Paolo d'Ancona and Erhard Aeschlimann, *Dictionnaire des miniaturistes du moyen âge et de la renaissance* (Milan, 1949), p. 18. The close relationship between artists and printers at Augsburg is well illustrated by Morgan MS. 782. "The drawings for the *Speculum* were more or less freely adapted by a woodcutter who later illustrated the edition published by Zainer at Augsburg in 1473. The representations of the Seven Virtues and Vices recur in the Bämler edition of the *Todsunden* [sic] of 1474 [PML CL 313]; the *Alexanderbuch* illustrations are copied in reverse in the woodcuts of the 1473 Bämler edition of that work and in the edition printed by Schott at Strassburg in 1493" (*Central European Manuscripts*, p. 70). See also note 125 below.

[14] The miniaturists worked indifferently for the producers of manuscripts or for the printers. "Ce qui donne surtout aux premiers incunables l'apparence du manuscrit, c'est la décoration entièrement exécutée à la main. . . . Pour les bibliophiles on a donc continué dans les livres imprimés un usage, auquel ils étaient habitués longtemps avant l'invention de l'art de l'imprimerie" (Leo S. Olschki, *Incunables illustrés imitant les manuscrits; le passage du manuscrit au livre imprimé* [Florence, 1914], pp. 5 and 7).

[15] On the influence of one craft upon the other, see Febvre and Martin, *op. cit.*, pp. 136-137. The effect of woodcuts upon the style of the later pen drawings is noted by Lehmann-Haupt (*Schwäb. Federzeich.*, p. 155). Even so famous a scribe as the celebrated Giovanni Marco Cinico (fl. 1463-

94) was not unwilling to be identified with a manuscript in which the illustrations were copied from a block book; cf. the Dyson Perrins *Arte de lo ben morire* manuscript (Perrins catalogue [see note 100 below], pp. 186-190, no. 79). Wegener (*op. cit.*, p. 324) notes the rise in the art of illuminating, during the last quarter of the fifteenth century, of the "Dilettantenarbeiten, die vielfach Kopien nach Buchholzschnitten sind."

[16] "Except for the trade in text-books at the university towns, the demand for books was so small that they were probably manufactured, as a rule, only to order. A scrivener or stationer could scarcely have afforded to risk putting his labour and materials into making books for stock, except, perhaps, in the case of such standard things as breviaries and primers" (Samuel Moore, "General Aspects of Literary Patronage in the Middle Ages," *The Library*, 3rd ser., IV [1913], 372-373).

[17] "Es gibt eine ganze Reihe solcher Handschriften, die den Einfluss des Auftraggebers, hauptsächlich in der Imitation fremder Stile, aber auch in der Wahl der Motive zeigen" (Wegener, p. 319).

[18] "Nach der Jahrhundertmitte ändert sich das Bild. . . Die Handschriftenillustration trat in den ersten Konkurrenzkampf mit dem Holzschnitt. Der neue Illustratorenstand wollte nicht mehr Massenarbeit sondern Qualitätsarbeit schaffen, und das Interesse und die Mitarbeit der Tafelmaler am Bildschmuck der Handschriften wurde stärker" (Wegener, p. 322).

[19] According to Lamberto Donati ("Divagazioni intorno alle 'Meditationes Johannis de Turrecremata' [1467]," *Maso Finiguerra*, IV [1939], 60), the Nürnberg copy of this book has three extra cuts (wanting in the other copies) pasted into the volume and colored similarly to those printed into it. These represent Adam and Eve in the Garden, the

Flight into Egypt, and Abraham and the Angels (figures 5, 7, and 9).

20 Occasionally one also finds professional work in the margins of manuscripts and early printed books; thus, Morgan MS. 819 (cf. *Treasures from the Pierpont Morgan Library*, p. 20, no. 27) and one of the Morgan copies (PML 44056) of Leo Baptista Alberti, *De re aedificatoria*, Florence: Nicolaus Laurentii, 29 Dec. 1485 (compare Frederick B. Adams, Jr., *Fourth Annual Report to the Fellows of the Pierpont Morgan Library* [New York, 1953], p. 29 and plate).

21 Cf. Febvre and Martin, *op. cit.*, p. 141. According to Olschki (*op. cit.*, p. 6), the woodcuts were "très souvent enluminées, sur la demande des amateurs, parce qu'elles étaient encore assez grossières d'exécution."

22 Compare the note to GW 5908: "Die Perg.-Ex. Angers BMun. und Paris BN hat Antoine Vérard illuminieren lassen. In dem dem König Karl VIII. gewidmeten Ex. Paris BN sind die ersten 2 1/2 Zeilen des Titels nach Rasur handschriftlich ersetzt durch die Worte: 'Le kalēdrier des bergiers ‖ nouuellemēt fait.' Die Druckermarke des Guy Marchant ist mit dem Wappen von Frankreich übermalt. Randleisten und Kolophon auf Bl. 89a sind ausradiert, der freie Raum übermalt; an der Stelle des Kolophons befindet sich die gemalte Verlegermarke des A. Vérard."

23 Macfarlane (*Vérard*, p. xii) writes that "in one respect he is without a rival—in the sumptuous illuminated copies on vellum, produced for his royal and other distinguished patrons. The Bibliothèque Nationale at Paris contains an astonishing number of these magnificent books, done for Charles VIII., Louis XI., and Anne of Brittany. Charles VIII.'s copy of the *Chroniques de France* contains, according to Van Praet, no less than 951 miniatures."

24 Olschki (*op. cit.*, pp. 6 and 15) noted that his copy of the Fust and Schoeffer Durandus of 6 October 1459 (GW

9101) had the colophon similarly scratched out. The same is true of the Bibliothèque Nationale copy (Vélin 127; Pellechet 4491).

25 "In King Henry VII's illuminated vellum copy [of H 11165] in the British Museum, Vérard, according to his wont, has erased the last twenty-seven words of the colophon, containing the date and printer's name and address" (Pierpont Morgan Catalogue, no. 530). A curious case is cited by BMC VIII:84 for its copy (IB. 41165) of the Boethius of 19 Aug. 1494 (GW 4580): "The presentation copy to King Henry VII; in the second line of the dedication on 2ª the words 'Charles. viii.' have been erased and 'Henry. vii.' substituted in pen-and-ink, and in the fourth line of the second column of the same 'Roy de frāce' has been similarly altered to 'Roy denglet're.'"

26 Cf. notes 22 and 23 above.

27 "The Museum copy of this book [*Vie et miracles de saint Martin*, 7 May 1496; H 10832], it should be added, bears all the marks—indifferently overpainted woodcuts and erased colophon—of having passed through the hands of Antoine Vérard, and it is thus without surprise that we note the name of Vérard in a list of booksellers established at Tours drawn from notarial records in the closing years of the century" (BMC VIII:lxxxvi).

28 "Certes, les premiers humanistes, ceux surtout de la fin du XVᵉ siècle et du début du XVIᵉ siècle, gens d'études avant tout, éprouvèrent à l'origine autant de dédain que les théologiens de la Sorbonne pour les livres illustrés: l'illustration n'était-elle pas un simple moyen d'instruire ceux qui étaient trop ignorants pour bien comprendre un texte?" (Febvre and Martin, *op. cit.*, p. 142). Recently it was pointed out by Edith G. Halpert, commenting on the American art at the Moscow exhibition (*New York Times*, Sunday, 2 August 1959, Section 2 [Drama], p. 15), "that with the high rate of literacy [Russians] boast, story-telling

paintings which the general public demands are an anachronism today."

29 One may well speculate on whether or not the grand, de luxe, illuminated manuscripts are books at all. They may well be works of art—or furniture, as little to be used as furniture on display in a museum. Clearly, the chief function of any book should be to perpetuate and disseminate learning and culture. If a volume filled with text and pictures fails to fulfill this function, whatever aesthetic values it may possess, it can hardly be thought to be performing the proper function of a book.

30 Wegener (*op. cit.*, pp. 320-321) maintains that the illustrations in the "Volkshandschriften" were not so much for decoration ("Schmuck") as for explanation, that is, they graphically depicted the text. They were often copied directly from standard models and have little claim to artistic merit. I have not elaborated on the fact that such illustration as the Accipies woodcuts served an advertising purpose.

31 "An Anonymous Latin Herbal in the Pierpont Morgan Library," *Osiris*, XI (1954), 259-266.

32 See the two articles by Victor Scholderer, "Red Printing in Early Books," *Gutenberg Jahrbuch 1958*, pp. 105-107, and "A Further Note on Red Printing in Early Books," *Gutenberg Jahrbuch 1959*, pp. 59-60, and works cited there.

33 Ferdinand Geldner ("Das 'Missale speciale' [bisher 'Constantiense' genannt], liturgie- und typengeschichtlich neu gesehen, "*Börsenblatt für den deutschen Buchhandel*, XV [1959], 285-293) seeks to establish that the Missal was not specially intended for the diocese of Constance but for the use of several dioceses: "für das Gebiet des Hochrheins bestimmt gewesen zu sein—ohne Rücksicht auf Diözesangrenzen" (p. 291).

34 Item 232 in the list provided by the Kommission and

printed by Hellmut Lehmann-Haupt, *Peter Schoeffer*, pp. 107-123.

[35] For the red printing in the Gutenberg Bible, see Schwenke's *Ergänzungsband*, p. 41; for that in the Psalters, see Masson, *Mainz Psalters*, pp. 25-30.

[36] The red printing in the Missal is discussed by Otto Hupp, *Gutenbergs erste Drucke* (Munich, 1902), pp. 17-27, and by Sir Irvine Masson, "The Dating of the *Missale speciale Constantiense*," *The Library*, 5th ser., XIII (1958), 97-99.

[37] Both Colard Mansion and William Caxton printed red and black at the same pull of the press, according to Blades, I, 43-44, and 54-55, though it was left for L. A. Sheppard (*New Light on Caxton*) to establish that *Les quatre dernières choses* was printed by the Englishman, not by the Belgian. Caxton also used the two-pull method (Blades, I, 55). Aldus Manutius seems to have used both methods; see my "Notes on two Incunabula printed by Aldus Manutius," *Papers of the Bibliographical Society of America*, XXXVI (1942), 22-23.

[38] Faulty register suggests that the Missal printer used a different two-pull technique, while Hupp (see note 36 above) has demonstrated that he employed a different single-pull method. See the further discussion of this in my "Another View on the Dating of the *Missale speciale Constantiense*," *The Library*, 5th ser., XIV (1959), 8-9.

[39] Sander (*Le livre à figures italien*, IV, xxx) recounts the amusing story of the creation of the "graveur Guerino, dit Meschi, qui exerçait son art vers 1495 à Florence." He writes: "Voilà ce qu'on lit dans un livre de référence très sérieux, très volumineux, qui traite de l'art et des artistes. Comment l'auteur a-t-il découvert ce Guerino? C'est bien simple: un fameux roman de chevalerie italien s'appelle Guerrino detto il Meschino (Guerrino dit le Meschin). Une des innombrables éditions de ce roman porte comme frontispice la figure du chevalier et, à droite, tout au bas

de la page, ce titre: Guerrino ditto Meschin.' Un historien de l'art a pris ce titre pour la signature du graveur et voilà né un 'nouvel ancien graveur florentin': Guerrino, aussi nommé Meschi." The authorship of the work is usually assigned to Andrea di Jacopo de' Mengabotti da Barberino in Valdelsa (c. 1370—c. 1431); cf. Natalino Sapegno, *Storia letteraria d'Italia, il Trecento* (Milan, 1948), p. 608, and Vittorio Rossi, *Storia letteraria d'Italia, il Quattrocento* (Milan, 1953), p. 416. The fifteenth-century editions are listed under GW 1643-53.

[40] "The Decoration of Early Mainz Books," *Magazine of Art*, XXXI (1938), 579-581.

[41] Cf. note 119 for Chapter II.

[42] William H. Schab, Catalogue No. 6, item 64, plate X.

[43] For an account of his life and his books, see Victor Scholderer, "Hilprand Brandenburg and his Books," *The Library*, 5th ser., IV (1949-50), 196-201.

[44] Devices suspended from boughs are discussed by George D. Painter, "Michael Wenssler's Devices and their Predecessors," *Gutenberg Jahrbuch 1959*, pp. 211-219.

[45] See Wilhelm L. Schreiber, "Die Anfänge des Buntfarbendrucks," *Gutenberg Jahrbuch 1928*, pp. 87-88.

[46] "Ninium [*sic*]. rote dint. est color rubeus quo depingi solent littere capitales" (Brack, *Vocabularius rerum*, PML CL 354, folio liiij^v). Wattenbach (*op. cit.*, p. 244) points out that the use of red is very ancient indeed, having been used by the early Egyptians.

[47] See the chapter "The Two-Colour Initials" in Masson, *Mainz Psalters*, pp. 50-58.

[48] On the early use of gold, see Wattenbach, *op. cit.*, pp. 251-261. "Goldschrift war schon im Alterthum beliebt" (p. 251). Some copies of Erhard Ratdolt's Euclid (Venice: 25 May 1482—GW 9428) have the dedicatory letter printed in gold; for example, the presentation copies at Augsburg SB, London BM, Munich SB, and Paris BN.

NOTES

[49] Compare Frederick B. Adams, Jr., *Fourth Annual Report to the Fellows of the Pierpont Morgan Library* (New York, 1953), p. 23; Konrad Haebler, *Handbuch der Inkunabelkunde* (Leipzig, 1925), p. 110; and the present writer's "A Volume from the Library of Dr. Nicolaus Pol," *Gutenberg Jahrbuch 1954*, pp. 147-151.

[50] See notes 35 and 38 above.

[51] Marginal instructions for the illuminator are often to be found in manuscripts; thus in Morgan MS. 389 and in the University of Pennsylvania Turrecremata manuscript (MS Lat. 37.—Donati, p. 53); so also in MS. Royal 19. D. 1 (see note 76 below).

[52] According to Ivins (*Artistic Aspects*, p. 38), the 1485 *Sphaera mundi* by Johannes de Sacro Busto, printed at Venice by Erhard Ratdolt (HC 14111; PML CL 863), contains "the earliest woodcuts (in this case diagrams only) to be printed in three colors." The Morgan copy of the Johannes de Ketham, *Fasciculo di medicina*, Venice: J. and G. de Gregoriis, 5 Feb. 1493, "is one of the copies in which the woodcut of the Dissection is printed in four colours: red, black, yellow and green" (Morgan Catalogue, II, 79, no. 355).

[53] For such work, see Frederick B. Adams, Jr., *Sixth Annual Report to the Fellows of the Pierpont Morgan Library* (New York, 1955), pp. 23-24.

[54] Cf. Henry Meier, "Woodcut Stencils of 400 Years Ago," *Bulletin of the New York Public Library*, XLII (1938), 10-19. So late as 1521, the *Cronica cronicarum*, Paris: Jacques Ferrebouc for Jean Petit and François Regnault (PML Acc. No. 25650) had its ninety-two woodcuts of Biblical scenes, portraits of kings, and views of cities colored by means of stencils; consult Howard C. Levis, *Notes on the Early British Engraved Royal Portraits* (London, 1917), pp. 215-219.

[55] Cf. Ivins, *Artistic Aspects*, p. 38. In commenting on the

initials found in the 1471 Jenson edition of Cornelius Nepos, Pollard remarked (Morgan Catalogue, no. 287): "These initials, like the woodcut borders found in other Venetian books of 1470-1472, exist in only a few copies, having been stamped in, after the book was printed, by hand pressure."

[56] Febvre and Martin (*op. cit.*, p. 141) maintain that the Venetians deliberately made use "des encadrements gravés dont le dessin sert de canevas à un peintre," but to the writer it seems likely that these were mostly not intended to be colored, save perhaps in the case of the vellum copies. These borders very closely parallel those found in manuscripts of the same date; e.g., the border in the *Privilegi dei Montefeltro* (Archivio Segreto Vaticano, AA. Arm. E. 123, f.1^r, reproduced in *La Bibliofilia*, LX [1958], 209).

[57] Ivins (p. 25) insists that the charm of the Anton Sorg illustration "such as it is, is to be sought primarily in their painting, for most of them had their woodcuts cheerily and gaudily daubed up with simple and childlike pigments." In early days the Briefmaler occasionally undertook "die Bemalung von Holzschnitten," and this subsequently became an important part of their business (Wilhelm L. Schreiber, "Die Briefmaler und ihre Mitarbeiter," *Gutenberg Jahrbuch 1932*, pp. 53-54). The coloring of Canon Cuts in the Missals was especially frequent (see Karl Schottenloher, *Die liturgischen Druckwerke Erhard Ratdolts aus Augsburg 1485-1522* [Mainz, 1922]). Nevertheless, collectors of our own day prefer to obtain uncolored woodcuts.

[58] The vellum copies lent themselves particularly to elaborate illumination, such as was usually reserved for vellum manuscripts. The three incunabula (nos. 608, 633, and 656) included in the "Mostra storica nazionale della miniatura" (*Catalogo* [Florence, 1954]) were vellum copies.

[59] One sometimes meets with mixed copies, containing both

vellum and paper leaves (viz., the Graz copy [Signatur IV. 9717] of the 1473 Schoeffer edition of the *Decretals* [HC 7999]; cf. Ferdinand Eichler, "Zwei illuminierte Wiegendrucke aus der Bibliothek der Georgsritter in Mill-statt," *Gutenberg Jahrbuch 1939,* pp. 121-127). The Bod-leian copy of the Fust and Schoeffer *Canon missae* is bound into a paper copy of the 1493 *Missale Moguntinum* (De Ricci, *Premières impressions,* pp. 64 and 68). In the Morgan copy (Acc. No. 49915) of the Liège Missal, Paris: Wolf-gang Hopyl for Franciscus Byrckman, 1 Sept. 1513, the sheet at the beginning of the Canon is printed on vellum. Manuscripts having vellum leaves as the outside and innermost sheets of a quire, thereby enclosing other paper sheets, are of common occurrence. This was a device to facilitate and strengthen the sewing of the quires in binding.

60 *Catalogue des livres imprimés sur vélin de la Bibliothèque du Roi* (Paris, 1822-28).

61 *Catalogue des livres imprimés sur vélin qui se trouvent dans les bibliothèques tant publiques que particulières* (Paris 1824-28).

62 See above, notes 13 and 102 of Chapter II.

63 The reprint of Andrew Borde's *The Fyrst Boke of the In-troduction of Knowledge* of about 1562, issued by Richard and Arthur Lane in 1814, consisted of 120 paper copies and four vellum ones (cf. my "Some Remarks on a Nineteenth-century Reprint," *Papers of the Bibliographical Society of America,* XLI [1947], 53-59). According to a note on the back of the title of the 1907 Morgan catalogue, the printing consisted of 170 paper copies and five on vellum.

64 For a transcript of the inscriptions, see De Ricci, *Premières impressions,* p. 29.

65 Cf. William H. Schab, Catalogue 23, no. 7, where the book is dated "before 24 June 1468." Jacobus Carpentarius dated his statement "about" the Feast of the Decollation of St. John the Baptist. This takes place on August 29th, the

Nativity falls on June 24th. Consult Adriano Cappelli, *Cronologia, Cronografia, e Calendario Perpetuo* (Milan, 1930), p. 136.

[66] See von Klemperer in *Gutenberg Jahrbuch 1927*, 50-52.

[67] According to BMC II:330.

[68] Wattenbach, *op. cit.*, p. 361. In the earliest English printing, such initials were not supplied in the spaces left empty by the printer. "Now, while in contemporary French, Italian, and Low Country books such spaces were often filled with the most gracefully designed and beautifully illuminated initials, rich in scrollwork and foliage, and ornamented with coats of arms or miniatures, there is not, so far as I know, any early English book in existence containing any attempt at such decoration. As a rule, the spaces were left blank as they came from the printer" (Duff, *Caxton*, p. 36).

[69] A curious case concerns the *editio princeps* of Euclid (Venice: Ratdolt, 25 May 1482). According to GW 9428, the printed initials in the vellum copies differ (at the beginning) from those in the paper copies. This is an excellent example of the trouble the printers were willing to go to in order to "pretty up" their productions. Incidentally, these initials are also part of Ratdolt's stock, despite the contrary assertion under Pell. 4630A.

[70] On this point, see Wattenbach, *op. cit.*, p. 345.

[71] An unusual instance is cited in Bernard M. Rosenthal's Catalogue IX (Summer, 1959), p. 9, item 34, and illustration on p. 50: the large initials were painted on small slips of paper which were then pasted into the manuscript. A manuscript by Molitor (Munich, Cgm 252) has printed initials pasted into it; cf. Wehmer, *Ne Italo*, p. 160 and Abb. 1.

[72] For the possible printing of initials into manuscripts by M. Zuane de Biaxo de Bologna at Venice as early as 1446, see Sander, *op. cit.*, IV, xiv. This practice is cited, without giving instances, by Febvre and Martin, *op. cit.*, p. 53.

Manuscripts Laon 106 and 427 (Édouard Fleury, *Les manuscrits à miniatures de la Bibliothèque de Laon* [Laon, 1863], II, 3-7 and 138-139) and a Seneca manuscript in the Vatican (Albert Lecoy de la Marche, *Les manuscrits et la miniature* [Paris, n. d.], p. 317) have initials stamped into them, the Laon manuscripts being as early as the thirteenth century. As late as 1499 (according to Wattenbach, p. 373), the monastery of Benediktbeuern bought seventeen "messing illuminier mödl" for the purpose of stamping such initials.

[73] Wehmer, *Ne Italo cedere videamur*, p. 160.

[74] Cf. Alfred W. Pollard, "The Woodcut Designs for Illumination in Venetian Books, 1469-73," *Bibliographica*, III (1897), 122-128. The "white-vine" design, often met with in incunabula from Venice, is equally common in manuscripts; cf. John Plummer, *Manuscripts from the William S. Glazier Collection* (New York, 1959), p. 26, no. 38 (Glazier MS. 22).

[75] Ivins (*Artistic Aspects*, p. 39) has pointed out that the border in the Herodotus, printed at Venice by the De Gregoriis in 1494 (HC 8472; PML CL 891), "has been more looked at and more emulated by designers for the press and for advertising purposes than any other" in modern times. He also remarks (p. 40) that "the Ovid of 1497 became the favorite pattern-book of the makers of the elaborately painted and decorated Venetian marriage chests and of the painters and decorators of the *maiolica* dishes that are among the loveliest and most charming of the minor works of industrial art of the Italian Renaissance."

[76] Manuscripts could be illuminated both before binding and after the binder had completed his work. Graham Pollard ("The Company of Stationers before 1557," *The Library*, 4th ser., XVIII [1937], 14) asserts that "a book cannot be illuminated after it is bound, because the paper or vellum will not lie flat." Nevertheless, D. J. A. Ross, in his study

of MS. Royal 19. D. 1 ("Methods of Book-Production in a XIVth Century French Miscellany," *Scriptorium*, VI [1952], 67), finds that "we have here evidence, which is not lacking elsewhere, of the fact that books were usually bound and not still in sheets or quires when they reached the illuminator." On pp. 65-66, he discusses the marginal notes (and occasionally even rough sketches) found in the margins to guide the miniaturist.

[77] Febvre and Martin, *op. cit.*, p. 153, also consider the "reliures de luxe, objets d'art réservés à une minorité de princes et de bibliophiles" as being beyond the scope of their investigation into "l'apparition du livre."

[78] Compare Kirchhoff, *Handschriftenhändler*, p. 11.

[79] On this point, see Hermann Knaus, "Über Verlegereinbände bei Schöffer," *Gutenberg Jahrbuch 1938*, pp. 97-108, and my own "The Binding of Books Printed by William Caxton," *Papers of the Bibliographical Society of America*, XXXVIII (1944), 1-8, together with the works cited in these articles. The fact that one not infrequently meets with quires from one book bound into another by the same printer indicates that the sheets were stored unbound as delivered by the pressman and that these misbound copies were probably bound at the press. BMC VIII:166 makes this interesting comment on the 1495 Tréperel edition of Gerson's *Opus tripartitum,* in French: "In this copy, as in the copy at Auxerre described by Pellechet-Polain (no. 5202), the place of quire B is taken by a copy of quire B of an edition of Raoul de Montfiquet, Exposition de l'oraison dominicale" printed in the same type as the Gerson. This seems to suggest that *both* copies were bound at the same place, namely the press. [Incidentally, the BMC here prints "tripertitum" for one of the very few misprints that can be cited from this remarkable work]. Consult also the writer's "The Edition of the 'Ditz moraulx des philosophes' Printed at Paris by Michel le Noir," *Gutenberg*

Jahrbuch 1950, pp. 182-185. If misbound books of this sort stem from the office of the original printer, then the contemporary bindings are valuable as evidence for what the publisher thought his products should look like.

80 The list of the unbound books in Clare College Library in 1496 totalled no fewer than eighty-seven items (Hunt, *Medieval Inventories of Clare,* 119-121). Johannes Sintram apparently kept his manuscripts unbound (cf. Theodore C. Petersen, *Speculum,* XX [1945], 75). Febvre and Martin (*op. cit.,* p. 155) also express the view that dealers kept their stock of printed books in sheets, and not in bound form.

81 See note 76 above.

82 Compare Rudolf Juchhoff, "Johann Veldener in Löwen als Buchdrucker und Buchbinder," *Gutenberg Jahrbuch 1933,* pp. 43-48.

83 *Verzeichniss der Handschriften der Stiftsbibliothek von St. Gallen* (Halle, 1875), p. 193, no. 602.

84 It is not surprising that binders took to printing; they had made use of movable type since 1436 (Wattenbach, *op. cit.,* p. 390). It has been recorded that Keller bound some fifty-seven books, all but one being printed within the years 1471-76 and thus having been produced prior to his own work at the press (1479-86); the remaining volume was published in 1488, after he had himself given up printing. See Ernst Kyriss, "Der Augsburger Drucker Ambrosius Keller als Buchbinder," *Gutenberg Jahrbuch* 1952, pp. 176-179. The Lapi family of Bologna was closely connected with the manufacture of books: Paolo had been a miniaturist, his son Domenico was both a miniaturist and a printer, and Domenico's son Giovanni Paolo became a binder (Sorbelli, *Stampa,* p. 36).

85 He certainly bound MS. Addit. 10106 of the British Museum. His tools were used, perhaps after Caxton's death, in the binding of College of Arms Young MS. 72. Since a fragment of Caxton printing is found in the (rebound)

Ebesham manuscript, Westminster Abbey MS. 29, this volume may also have been first bound by the "Caxton binder"; in turn, this would suggest that the binder worked close to, if not actually in, Caxton's printing office. Compare A. I. Doyle's article listed in note 112, Chapter I.

[86] The Rylands copy of Caxton's *Propositio Johannis Russell*, bound together with blank leaves used for manuscript entries (which continue on the blank pages of the incunable), was listed among the manuscripts in a 1807 sale as: "A work on theology and religion, with five leaves at the end a very great curiosity, very early printed on wooden blocks, or type" (Duff, *Caxton*, p. 44).

[87] "A Tudor 'Crosse Rowe,' " *Journal of English and Germanic Philology*, LVIII (1959), 248-250, where the earlier numbers are listed. On Sammelbände, see Lynn Thorndike, "The Problem of the Composite Manuscript," *Miscellanea Giovanni Mercati*, VI, 93-104. It is really remarkable how few manuscripts contain only a single text. See also p. 47 and notes 51-53, Chapter II. A Sammelband has been aptly called a "library in parvo"; for such a book, see my "Sir John Paston's *Grete booke*, a fifteenth-century 'Best-Seller,' " *Modern Language Notes*, LVI (1941), 345-351.

[88] The recent article by Franz Unterkircher ("Die Grolier-Einbände der Österreichischen Nationalbibliothek," *Gutenberg Jahrbuch 1959*, pp. 249-258) brings supplemental information which does not change the over-all picture.

[89] The catalogue of the painted Renaissance books in the *Bibliothèque Pillone* (Paris, 1957) also provides some interesting figures. Thirty-one of the sixty-three entries (almost exactly half of the total) under "Livres reliés au quinzième siècle" are classical works, including but one vernacular book among the incunables. Of the ninety-four sixteenth-century books, only twenty-six are classics, some of these being in the vernacular, as well as fifteen other vernacular books.

90 *Researches concerning Jean Grolier, his Life and his Library* (New York, 1907).

91 See *The History of Bookbinding, 525-1950 A.D., an Exhibition held at the Baltimore Museum of Art, November 12, 1957 to January 12, 1958* (Baltimore, 1957). I have counted sixteen classical texts (including one Boethius here), nine volumes of legal and historical content, four of popular vernacular texts, nine of various Latin writings, and seven volumes of interest to humanists.

92 Ernst P. Goldschmidt, *Gothic and Renaissance Bookbindings exemplified and illustrated from the Author's Collection* (London, 1928). Three classics, seven popular texts in Latin, six in law and history, and two humanist works complete the total.

93 Febvre and Martin, *op. cit.*, p. 152, point out that the early "working books," including those of the seventeenth century, were much more sturdily and attractively bound than is the custom today. These were not, however, encased in "reliures de luxe" of the sort that appeals to collectors of our own times.

94 "Le livre de très grand luxe, véritable oeuvre d'art, destinée à être regardée et non pas lue comme les somptueux volumes appartenant au duc de Berry" (Febvre and Martin, p. 21).

95 *Babbitt* (New York, Grosset & Dunlap, no date), pp. 92, 214.

96 Such work has been termed "xylo-chirographique" by Wilhelm L. Schreiber, who has described a number of such works in his *Manuel de l'amateur de la gravure sur bois et sur métal au XVe siècle* (Leipzig, 1891-1911), IV, 90, 231, 321, 418.

97 Compare, for example, Domenico Fava, "Libri membranacei stampati in Italia nel Quattrocento," *Gutenberg Jahrbuch 1937*, pp. 55-78.

98 Sander (*op. cit.*, IV, xii) refers to the celebrated volume in the Biblioteca Classense, Ravenna: "dans ce manuscrit

traitant de sujets juridiques, le premier propriétaire a inséré quarante xylographies," with bibliographical references to the pertinent literature on the subject.

[99] Printed books also, of course, had woodcuts pasted into them, particularly in the case of the earliest productions. The Morgan copy of the *Missale speciale* (*? Constantiense*) has a woodcut of the Crucifixion inserted opposite the beginning of the Canon; at the same place the St. Paul copy of the *Missale abbreviatum* has a "Reiberdruck" of this theme. For further details, see my "The Constance Missal and two Documents from the Constance Diocese," *Papers of the Bibliographical Society of America*, L (1956), 371-372, n. 5. An unusual "pasteprint" of the Crucifixion has been attached to the leaf facing the Canon in the Morgan copy of the *Missale Romanum*, Nürnberg: Georg Stuchs, 1484 (HC 11384; PML CL 439). On such prints, see Thomas O. Mabbott, "Pasteprints and Sealprints," *Metropolitan Museum Studies*, IV (1932), 55-75.

[100] Sir George Warner, *Descriptive Catalogue of Illuminated Manuscripts in the Library of C. W. Dyson Perrins* (Oxford, 1920).

[101] Cf. the Dyson Perrins sale catalogue, part I (London, Sotheby & Co., 9 December 1958, p. 72). BM Addit. 15712 ("Von dem Abentessen unsers Herren Jhesu Christi") is described as: "On paper, written in the year 1459; and illustrated with twenty-six rude wood engravings, colored, which have been pasted down in the blank spaces left by the scribe."

[102] Karl Küp, "A Fifteenth-Century Girdle Book," *Bulletin of the New York Public Library*, XLIII (1939), 471-484. For other uses to which such woodcuts were put, see the same writer's "A Fifteenth-Century Cofferet," *Renaissance News*, IX (1956), 14-19.

[103] Consult Lehmann-Haupt, *Schwäb. Federzeich.*, pp. 117, 119, and 193-194.

[104] Carleton Brown and Rossell Hope Robbins, *The Index of Middle English Verse* (New York, 1943, no. 3584): "Printed with prose additions in 1449." This is obviously a misprint for the 1499 De Worde edition (STC 5643).

[105] See the description given by Sir William A. Craigie in his edition for the Scottish Text Society, new series, vols. XIV and XVI (Edinburgh, 1923-25), pp. v-x.

[106] Cf. Hellmut Lehmann-Haupt, "Ein vollständiges Exemplar des xylo-chirographischen Antichrist," *Gutenberg Jahrbuch 1934*, pp. 69-71; Hans Holter, "Beispiele von Graphik in Handschriften," *Die graphischen Künste,* neue Folge, IV (1939), 41-46; and Christian von Heusinger, "Ein Neujahrsgruss auf das Jahr 1459," *Gutenberg Jahrbuch 1959*, pp. 36-40.

[107] For further discussion, see Eichler in *Gutenberg Jahrbuch 1939*, p. 121, and Kautzsch, p. 79 (cf. note 115, Chapter I).

[108] Fitz, *König Mathias Corvinus,* p. 136, and *Treasures from the Pierpont Morgan Library,* p. 27, no. 48.

[109] The illuminators seem to have suffered not at all from the introduction of the press, since more work was available for them than ever before (cf. Schreiber, *Briefmaler,* pp. 53-54). That there was some "wholesale" illuminating of Fust and Schoeffer publications would appear to be a proper deduction to be drawn from Adolph Goldschmidt's study (see pp. 72-74 above).

[110] The copies in Florence are described by Domenico Fava (*Gutenberg Jahrbuch 1937,* p. 60 and Fig. 1); the Morgan copy, formerly in the collections of Maffeo Pinelli, John Dent and Sir John Thorold (Syston Park), was elaborately bound by Roger Payne (PML CL 1167). The Cracherode copy in the British Museum (BMC VI:667; IB. 28002) is "imperfect, wanting the second leaf, which bore an illuminated border, etc.," and one wonders if it too might not have been decorated in a fashion similar to the Morgan and the two Florentine copies.

[111] "Sir John Fastolf's Manuscripts of the *Épître d'Othéa* and Stephen Scrope's Translation of this Text," *Scriptorium,* III (1949), p. 128, n. 35.

[112] A number of studies, of course, have already been cited for individual books and of haphazard groups, but what are needed are comprehensive investigations of series of related books. A characteristically valuable study of a single work is that by Franz Unterkircher, "Die Buchmalerei im Wiener Exemplar der ersten Deutschen Bibel von Mentelin 1466," *Gutenberg Jahrbuch 1955,* pp. 75-81.

[113] Bell (*Price of Books,* p. 319) states that "illumination does not appear to have been a very costly item in the production of theological and philosophical texts." He adds: "Much of this simple illuminating was done with the pen, and there was still no rigid distinction between scribe and illuminator" (p. 320).

[114] Wattenbach, *op. cit.,* p. 394. The Kraus Catalogue 88, item 46, describes a Gradual with the colophon: "Hoc opus scriptum notatum ac miniatum fuit penna et penello Cremone per me Ludouicum de gaçis ciuem Cremonensem." This, the only known work by this artist, is decorated by thirteen, handsomely executed, historiated initials.

[115] See above, note 58, Chapter II. Vérard was originally "a calligrapher and miniaturist and possessed a scriptorium catering for aristocratic patrons" (BMC VIII:xxvi). Lapi "is first heard of in 1470 in a document describing him as a 'miniatore'" (BMC VI:xxxiii). Zainer had been a member of the "Painters-guild" in Strassburg before moving to Ulm (Voulliéme, *Die deutschen Drucker,* p. 163).

[116] One finds human and animal figures in pen-work as marginal decoration (PML CL 23). According to Loren C. MacKinney ("Medical Illustrations in Medieval Manuscripts of the Vatican Library," *Manuscripta,* III [1959], 3-18 and 76-88), MSS. Chigi F. VIII. 188 and Pal. lat. 1066 have such rough medical illustrations. In the Yale copy of

GW 6798, a realistic "guillotine" scene has been sketched in alongside the appropriate lines in Cicero's *Philippic* 1.5. The copy of the *Ackermann von Böhmen* ([Bamberg: Albrecht Pfister, c. 1463]—GW 194) in the Bibliothèque Nationale (Réserve A 1646) has at the end a sketch of a Wild Woman holding a shield with the motto: "got giptz vnd nimptz."

[117] *Artistic Aspects*, p. 10. Proctor's opinion is cited on p. 8.

[118] Professionals, on occasion, inserted things into already printed books, as (for example) the Florentine Dante of 1481. It was intended to illustrate this edition with copper-plates, but only nineteen of these were completed. In some cases, these illustrations were printed into the volumes after the work on the letter-press had been accomplished; in other instances, the plates were used to print impressions on separate slips of paper which were then pasted into the volumes. For further details, see the Morgan Catalogue, no. 398; Mongan and Wolf, *The First Printers*, p. 59; and C. H. Rother, "Nicolaus Laurentii und seine Danteausgabe vom Jahre 1481," *Zeitschrift für Bücherfreunde*, neue Folge, XIII (1921), 78-80.

[119] For the essential differences between German and Italian illustration, see Sander, *op. cit.*, IV, xxi-xxiii, and Ivins, *Artistic Aspects*.

[120] "Nicht nur die Hs. wurde durch das gedruckte Buch verdrängt, auch die Federzeichnung durch den Bilddruck" (Kautzsch, *op. cit.*, p. 75).

[121] (Paris and Brussels, 1928). I have computed a few figures which may interest those scholars concerned with what texts were most frequently illustrated (at least, in so far as the manuscripts have survived to our day). In the Exhibition catalogue, *Les manuscrits à peintures en France du XIII*[e] *au XVI*[e] *siècle* (Paris, 1955), there are listed 362 items, of which 170 (almost forty-seven per cent.) are Bibles and liturgical books, and forty-two are religious and devotional

texts. There are 120 popular works in the list (with the biblical and liturgical works, this total amounts to eighty per cent. of the exhibition), together with nineteen scientific and eleven legal texts. In the Italian Exhibition which covered all centuries (see the catalogue *Mostra storica nazionale della miniatura* [Florence, 1954]), 732 items pertinent to our discussion were included, of which 386 (or fifty-three per cent.) were biblical and liturgical books. The next largest classification, formed of religious and devotional texts, reached a total of 103 entries (or fourteen per cent.). Popular and legal works both totalled exactly sixty-eight, with fifty-one classical volumes, forty-six scientific treatises and ten books of historical interest. Included in the historical category is the only school-book found suitable for the exhibition (no. 661), but a magnificent book it is, containing the works by Donatus and (Pseudo)-Cato, probably executed by Ambrogio de Predis for the use of Maximilian Sforza, the young son of Ludovico il Moro (Biblioteca Trivulziana MS. 2167).

[122] It has been pointed out by H. S. Bennett ("Science and Information in English Writings of the Fifteenth Century," *Modern Language Review*, XXXIX [1944], 1-8) and Donald B. Sands ("Caxton as a Literary Critic," *Papers of the Bibliographical Society of America*, LI [1957], 315) that the fifteenth-century Englishman was much concerned with straight, factual information, which did not easily lend itself to formal illumination.

[123] It has also been asserted that, except for Worcester, English book collectors of the fifteenth century were "indifferent to the physical appearance of their books" (Weiss in Wormald and Wright, *op. cit.*, p. 123). For an account of his library, see R. J. Mitchell, "A Renaissance Library: The Collection of John Tiptoft, Earl of Worcester," *The Library*, 4th ser., XVIII (1937), 67-83. For the magnificent Psalter and other manuscripts written for John, Duke of Bedford, see Eric G. Millar, "Fresh Materials for the Study of English Illumina-

tion," *Studies in Art and Literature for Belle da Costa Greene* (Princeton, 1954), pp. 286-294.

[124] Lehmann-Haupt (*Heritage of the Manuscript*, pp. 22-23) rightly calls attention to the "pathetic attempts to outdo the woodcuts" by the pen and to the fact that "some makers of block books, like some manuscript scribes, imitated the printed books."

[125] See, for example, Ferdinand Eichler, "Zwei illuminierte Wiegendrucke aus der Bibliothek der Georgsritter in Mill-statt," *Gutenberg Jahrbuch 1939*, 121-127. The Morgan copy of the Franciscus de Zabarellis, *Lectura super Clementinis*, Turin: Benedictis and Suigus, 23 Aug. 1492 (PML CL 1323), contains on signature a2 at the head of the text, a miniature in gold and colors which portrays the author as a Franciscan, lecturing from his book on a lectern. The volume had obviously been illuminated north of the Alps, and it bears the note of former ownership of the Franciscan Monastery of the Holy Cross at Würzburg. The illumination was considered to be sufficiently important so that the incunable was included in the exhibition of Central European manuscripts (16 Dec. 1957—12 Apr. 1958), though not being a manuscript it was excluded from the catalogue. A copy of the Schoeffer *Liber sextus Decretalium* of 1473 (GW 4853) was illuminated by Ludovicus Ravescot, who later became a printer in Louvain; cf. Sotheby sale, 11 April 1960, lot 1087. Lot 1123 in the same sale comprised a copy of the 1471 Schoeffer *Constitutiones* (GW 7081), with a miniature of Pope Clement V writing at his desk.

[126] GW 7580-7777. Cuts occur as follows: GW 7630, Lyon: Du Pré, 1493 (1 cut); GW 7652, Paris: Gering and Remboldt, 1499 (2); GW 7723, Nürnberg: Sensenschmidt and Frisner, 1475 (10); GW 7735, Nürnberg: Koberger, 1488 (10); GW 7776, Augsburg: Ratdolt, 1493 (1); and GW 7777, Augsburg: Zeissenmair, 1494 (1). A single

schematic cut is also found in GW 7653, Lyon: Jean de Vingle, 1500.

127 Schreiber 5050-54. A great many others were issued in the sixteenth century.

128 Schreiber 5168-71. The editions of the *Lehenrecht* (GW 7776-77) really belong in this group. The Morgan copy of the earlier edition (PML CL 384) is further decorated by being bound in the publisher's paper covers with a woodcut design, dated 1494. Such "bindings" are discussed by Leo Baer, *Holzschnitte auf Buchumschlägen aus dem XV. und der ersten Hälfte des XVI. Jahrhunderts* (Strassburg, 1936); William A. Jackson, "Printed Wrappers of the Fifteenth to the Eighteenth Centuries," *Harvard Library Bulletin*, VI (1952), 313-321; and Rudolf Hirsch, "The Decoration of a 1486 Book Wrapper and its Reappearance in 1531," *Studies in the Renaissance*, VI (1959), 167-174.

129 GW 8494-8566. The Italian edition is the *Diurnale Camaldulense*, Venice: Johann Emerich for Lucantonio Giunta, 28 Feb. 1497-8, GW 8511.

130 GW 5101-5518. The Würzburg Breviaries are listed under GW 5356-61.

131 See above, note 99, Chapter III.

132 Fava-Bresciano 121; PML CL 1229. The Morgan vellum copy is lavishly decorated, with borders, marginal figures, and illuminated initials. The arms on folio 65 are those of the Guevara family, and the volume may have been decorated for Pietro di Guevara, grand seneschal to Ferdinand I of Naples.

133 Hanns Bohatta, *Bibliographie der Livres d'heures . . . des XV. und XVI Jahrhunderts* (Vienna, 1924), p. 70, no. 187.

134 Now in the Pierpont Morgan Library, Acc. no. 18244. Michele Ghislieri (1504-1572) became Pope Pius V on 7 Jan. 1566. He was beatified in 1672 and was canonized in 1712, being one of the last Popes to be made a Saint.

[135] Statistics such as appear in this study must be treated with care. It is entirely up to the compiler whether he will treat a scientific classic as a work of science or as a classical text. Here they are treated in the former category. Similarly, can Boethius qualify as a classic? In this study, he is so considered, since the *De consolatione philosophiae* will fit into none of the other arbitrary classes selected for this analysis. There are many such problems, and no two estimates are likely to be quite the same.

[136] *Catalogue des incunables à figures imprimés en Allemagne, en Suisse, en Autriche-Hongrie et en Scandinavie* (Leipzig, 1910-11; vol. V of his *Manuel*).

[137] For further details, see my *Fifteenth Century Books and the Twentieth Century* (New York, 1952); "Authors and Incunabula," *Studies . . . for Belle da Costa Greene*, pp. 401-406; and "Iberian Incunabula in America," *The Library Quarterly*, XXIII (1953), 281-283. Statistics also appear in Febvre and Martin, *op. cit.*, p. 378 ff., but the results seem to differ considerably from my own findings. Among Hispanic illustrated books, there are some 254 non-Latin works against only 120 in that tongue.

[138] *El arte tipográfico en España durante el siglo XV* (Madrid, 1945-1954); consult also Konrad Haebler, *Bibliografía Ibérica del siglo XV* (The Hague, 1903-17).

[139] In Martin Kurz (*Handbuch der iberischen Bilddrucke des XV. Jahrhunderts* [Leipzig, 1931]), there are listed 372 entries but two of these (81a and b and 224a and b) are double entries. They may be classified as follows:

Science	23	Liturgical	25
Classical	21	*Expositio hymnorum*	9
Devotional	119	Indulgences	27
Law & Chronicles	51	Popular works	58
Schoolbooks/didactics	33	Hebrew books	8

[140] *Der Buchdruck Kölns bis zum Ende des fünfzehnten Jahrhunderts* (Bonn, 1903).

[141] *Der Bilderschmuck der Frühdrucke* (Leipzig, 1924-40; Vol. VIII: "Die Kölner Drucker").

[142] On the basis of Voulliéme's study of Cologne incunabula, Ivins (*Artistic Aspects,* p. 16) suggests that "the reading Germans of that time were interested in theology and the grammatical subjects of the medieval universities to the nearly complete exclusion of everything else." This somewhat overlooks the special nature of the booktrade in that city, which seems to have been completely under the control of the University. The University, in turn, was one of the last strongholds of scholastic learning. Soon after the turn of the century, Cologne's theological faculty became the butt for the satires of the writers of the *Epistolae obscurorum virorum;* cf. the introduction by Francis G. Stokes to his edition of the *Epistolae* (London, 1925, pp. xv-lxxiii, esp. p. xlvii). Nevertheless, Cologne printers issued at least a dozen Ciceros, half that number of Vergils, four Ovids, and nine Senecas, indicating that there was some demand for classical texts in the Rhenish capital. A quite different view is expressed by Victor Scholderer (BMC VII:xxxvii): "The contribution of the North to early printing is in many respects inferior to that of Italy, but it has at any rate this interest that it shows the Northern mind here and there definitely on the move; as Dr. Pollard has noted in the case of Germany, the book-trade of that country perceptibly reflects the increasing preoccupation of thoughtful men with new ideas in religion and points the way to the coming of the Reformation within a few decades. Whatever the qualities of the Italian incunabula, we cannot find in them any prefigurement of a new outlook on life."

[143] Printers were not above using a cut which had nothing to do with the text. Thus Ugo Rugerius used a cut of the Visitation in two editions of the *Formulario di epistole* and in a *Passione di Jesu Cristo* (Bühler nos. 6.A.15, 6.A.16, and 6.A.30; compare Domenico Fava, "L'illustrazione

182

libraria a Bologna nel Quattrocento," *Gutenberg Jahrbuch 1939*, p. 166). For the "Accipies" woodcuts, see: Robert Proctor, "The Accipies Woodcut" (in his *Bibliographical Essays* [London, 1905], pp. 1-12); W. L. Schreiber and P. Heitz, *Die deutschen Accipies und Magister cum discipulis-Holzschnitte* (Strassburg, 1908); Max J. Husung, "Magister cum discipulis- und Magister-Darstellungen auf Leder-schnitteinbänden des 15. Jahrhunderts," *Gutenberg Jahrbuch 1942/43*, pp. 412-424; etc.

[144] In view of the English indifference to the appearance of their manuscripts (see note 123 above), it is not surprising that only a handful of illustrated incunabula were issued there. On the other hand, the enormous production of *Books of Hours* and other illustrated liturgical volumes at Paris, which specialized in books of this sort, tends to give a distorted picture of the book illustration of the period, if statistics are based and conclusions are reached on the basis of the book-production in England or in the French capital.

[145] *University and Press in Bologna*, pp. 59-101. The total is reached by the inclusion of ten devotional and religious works, and a similar number of popular and vernacular texts, while only a single book represents, respectively, the classics and legal literature.

[146] *op. cit.*, IV, cxi-cxiv.

[147] *op. cit.*, IV, cxxxiv-cxxxv.

[148] Mariano Fava and Giovanni Bresciano, *La stampa a Napoli nel XV secolo* (Leipzig, 1911-12). Six classics and a similar number of devotional texts, and five books of a popular nature also were illustrated.

[149] Giovanni Gaye, *Carteggio inedito d'artisti dei secoli XIV. XV. XVI* (Florence, 1839-40), I, 267. There, Gaye makes the comment: "L'invezione [*sic*] della stanpa [*sic*] diventò una causa naturale, che l'arte del miniatore sul finire di questo secolo s'approssimava alla decadenza."

Index

INDEX